HUNTER TO HUNTED

SURVIVING HITLER'S WOLF PACKS

Diaries of a Merchant Navy Radio Officer, 1939-45

HUNTER TO HUNTED

SURVIVING HITLER'S WOLF PACKS

Alex Anderson

This book is dedicated to the everlasting memory of my dearly loved parents, John Blair Anderson and Janet Thomson Plenderleith.

Contents

Part I - Antarctic Whaling Expedition (1939 – 1940)

Part II – North Atlantic Convoys (1940 – 1945)

Vessels Author Served On

Christian Salvesen Co.

SS Salvestria 16th October – 5th December 1939
(Sunk by enemy action 27 July 1940)

MV Sirra 5th December 1939 – 16th March 1940
(Converted to RN Minesweeper (HMT Sirra) 1940-46)

SS New Sevilla 16th March – 2nd May 1940
(Sunk by enemy action 20 September 1940)

SS Peder Bogen 23rd May 1940 – 28th October 1941
(Sunk by enemy action 23rd March 1942)

SS Sourabaya 10th November 1941 – 31st August 1942
(Sunk by enemy action 27th October 1942)

SS Saluta 20th November 1942 – 15th October 1943

Netherlands Shipping & Transport Co.

SS Winsum 10th December 1943 – 8th October 1945

Author Biography

He was born Alexander (Alex.) Anderson at Spittalfield Schoolhouse, Perthshire, Scotland in 1920 to School Headmaster John Blair Anderson and his wife Janet (Plenderleith). Educated at Perth Academy before attending Dundee Wireless College, the author graduated in 1939 with a Postmaster General's Certificate in Radio Telegraphy(1st class). Employed firstly by the Christian Salvesen shipping company of Leith, Scotland, he left home aged 19 years to take up the position of third R/O on the New Sevilla Whaling Expedition, 1939-40 Season. Following the rigours of the Antarctic, he was thrust into the longest campaign of WWII, the North Atlantic convoys.

In total, he would serve on seven vessels, four of which were subsequently lost to enemy action. Discharged from War Service on 28th November 1945, he set up home in Crieff, Perthshire where he ran a successful Radio & TV business, and later, a B&B guesthouse with wife Betty. His final wish was the publication of his manuscript which, although only representing six of his eighty years, became his life's work.

Acknowledgements

I wish to record my heartfelt gratitude to my dear wife Betty and our sons Bill and Iain for their unrelenting encouragement, care and support through recent difficult times, which I pray will lead to the realisation of my dream for publication of this book.

SS Salvestria, SS Sourabaya, SS Saluta, SS New Sevilla and SS Peder Bogen images courtesy of UoE Centre for Research Collections.

SS Winsum image courtesy of Collection het Scheepvaartmuseum, Amsterdam.

'Conning tower of German submarine 190, showing Schnorkel mast and White Ensign flying over Kreigsmarine flag' courtesy of Library and Archives Canada/Department of National Defence fonds/a145577.

Convoy image courtesy of T&G Jones (www.rhiw.com).

Illustrations

Abbreviations

AB	Able Seaman
AKA	Also Known As
DBS	Distressed British Seaman
DF	Direction Finder
DG	Degaussing (Cables)
ETA	Estimated Time of Arrival
Flf	Floating factory
GLD	Land's End Radio (Call Sign)
GMT	Greenwich Mean Time
GOC	General Officer Commanding
HMS	His Majesty's Ship
HMT	His Majesty's Trawler
LTH	Leith Harbour Radio (Call sign)
MBE	(Member, etc) British Empire Medal
MN A/A	Merchant Navy Anti-Aircraft (Gunnery)
MV	Motor Vessel
OBE	(Officer, etc) British Empire Medal
OS	Ordinary Seaman
PCS	Position, Course & Speed
POW	Prisoner of War
RAF	Royal Air Force
RMS	Royal Mail Ship

RN	Royal Navy
R/O	Radio Officer
ROK	Received Okay
RRRR	Armed Raider Sighting (Distress Call)
SOS	Save Our Souls
SS	Screw Steamer (aka Steam Ship)
SSS	Submarine Sighting (Distress Call)
US	United States (of America)
USS	United States Ship
VCE	Cape Race Radio (Call Sign)
W/Op	Wireless Operator
W/T	Wireless Telegraph(y)
ZBH	Grytviken Radio (Call Sign)

Introduction

My story begins on 14th June 1939 when, aged nineteen, I received a telegram.

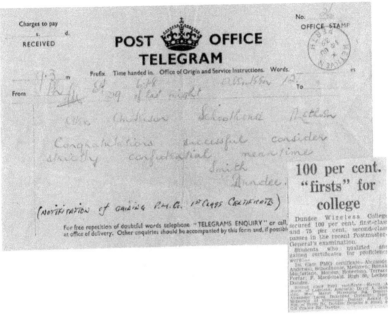

Fig.1 Telegram notifying PMG Cert. Pass & Newspaper Report

The local paper simultaneously carried the same story - '100 percent 'firsts' for College'. I was one of a full complement of 1st Class certificate passes. It meant I had successfully passed my exams and gained the 'Certificate of Proficiency (First Class) in Radiotelegraphy' from the Postmaster General. I was now authorised to operate radiotelegraph and radio-telephone apparatus as a first-class operator on-board a British vessel. Finally, the climax to my training at the Dundee Wireless College, class of 1939.

DUNDEE COLLEGE, 1939

Fig.2 Dundee Wireless College 1939 (Author circled)

'This is it,' I thought to myself. *'Now, the world is my oyster.* I will be able to travel the world, visiting all the wonderful and exotic places that I have read and dreamt about. After a few years, I will return, open my own business and settle down.' How easily I seemed to map out my perfect life plan in only a few minutes of receiving that telegram, now clutched in my hand.

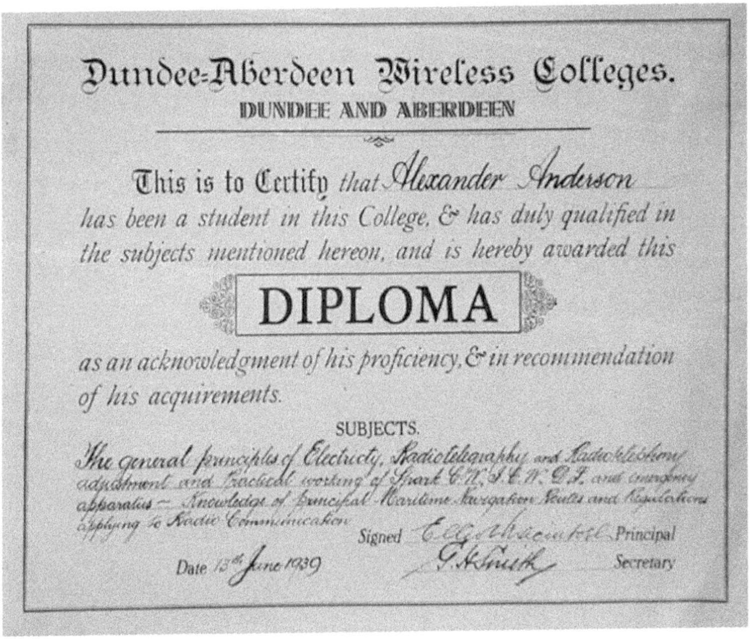
Dundee-Aberdeen Wireless Colleges.
DUNDEE AND ABERDEEN

This is to Certify that Alexander Anderson has been a student in this College, & has duly qualified in the subjects mentioned hereon, and is hereby awarded this

DIPLOMA

as an acknowledgment of his proficiency, & in recommendation of his acquirements.

SUBJECTS.

The general principles of Electricity, Radiotelegraphy and Radiotelephony adjustment and Practical working of Spark C.W., I.C.W., D.F., and emergency apparatus — Knowledge of principal Maritime Navigation Rules and Regulations applying to Radio Communication

Signed Principal

Secretary

Date 13th June 1939

Fig.3 PMG Radio Telegraphy Certificate (1st Class)

Little did I know that I would begin my life at sea on the brink of a world war, and finish some six years later, at its end. I would never reach those South Sea Islands of my boyhood dreams, although I would, by way of some compensation, get to set foot in the Dutch West Indies.

Being in the Caribbean, and occasionally forming part of our future cargo itinerary, this was the most exotic that my destinations were ever likely to be. It would be the vast Atlantic Ocean that would, more or less, become my 'goldfish bowl' during those turbulent six years. This did not mean that I wouldn't experience the extraordinary, the bizarre or the unforgettable.

After gaining my diploma, I was impatient to get my first ship. Weeks and months passed without an offer, and I reached desperation stage. Willing to abandon all thoughts of sea travel, I approached the RAF. After an interview, however, they said my qualifications were actually more than they required at that time. I was duly advised to be patient and await the offer of a post for which I had been specifically trained.

Part I

Antarctic Whaling Expedition
(1939 – 1940)

"None of it was easily earned.
The conditions were brutal. Ice often clogged
the rigging and individual catching boats were
known to founder in the steep seas of
the Southern Ocean."

(https://www.bbc.co.uk/news/magazine-27734930.)

Chapter 1 - SS Salvestria

Fig.4 SS Salvestria

It was the 13th of October 1939 ... and it was a Friday!

On this rather ominous day, four months after receiving my Diploma, my second long-awaited telegram arrived. What a surprise it turned out to be. I was being offered a position as Radio Officer (R/O) attached to an Antarctic Whaling Expedition by Christian Salvesen of Leith. All thoughts of exotic locations having now diminished, I immediately wired back my acceptance.

Next morning, I received a telephone call giving me the full details. I had to get a Doctor's Fitness Report, then travel to their offices in Leith on Monday morning, *'complete with kit, including warm clothing'*. I would be sailing down to South Georgia in the Falklands on the factory ship SS Salvestria. During the three-month fishing season, I would be serving as Radio Officer on one of the small whale catchers. The whole voyage would last for at least six months.

On Saturday morning, my mother was helping out at a church sale of work but was rushing off to Perth (our nearest large town) afterwards, to procure some extra items of warmer clothing for me. This included my first introduction to 'long johns'. On that and the following day, I met with some friends to say my short-notice goodbyes.

Later that Sunday evening, my father took me aside. He told me that I was about to embark on a *'great adventure'*, which few would be fortunate enough to experience, and many would envy. It was very important, therefore, that I try to keep a diary of events as they unfolded. To encourage me, he handed over three small school jotters and pencils. Little did either of us know that, because of subsequent acute war-time shortages, I would soon be opening up old envelopes to have something on which to write and continue my diary entries.

On the other hand, maternal advice came in the form of a small Bible that my mother placed in my case. At the top of the inside page, she had written my name, the date *'15 October 1939'* and a simple reference, *'Prov. 3.6'* – nothing else. I leave it to the reader to look it up, but I can say that it has been imprinted on my memory ever since.

The next morning, I left home at 7:45 a.m. accompanied by my father, who would travel to Leith with me. We were driven to the Perth railway station by Tom Donald, a joiner from Scone, who would later become my brother-in-law on marrying my younger sister Mary. Whilst on the train, I glanced through a newspaper and happened to see my horoscope which, prophetically, included the words, 'A good day for travelling'. I cannot say, however, that I was in agreement with that statement by the end of the day.

We arrived at Salvesen's Bernard Street office in Leith at 9:45 a.m. After signing the contract papers, I was on a monthly salary of £11 15s (shillings) per month, with an extra 15s per month when serving on the small whale catcher. I found to my surprise that the Salvestria was not lying at Leith, as I had expected. It was on the River Tyne at South Shields, just over the border in northeast England. As a result, I was duly issued with a rail voucher. This would provide me with a seat in one of two or three carriages reserved for crew members serving on various ships taking part in the same expedition.

On leaving the office, I met another lad (MacDonald) who had been at the Wireless Training College with me and who was also going on the same expedition. However, he had turned up without his kit, so would not be joining the ship until the following day. The train for Newcastle left at 1 p.m. As I said goodbye to my father, I could not help but feel the emotion of the situation welling up inside me. With my last link with home now severed, it

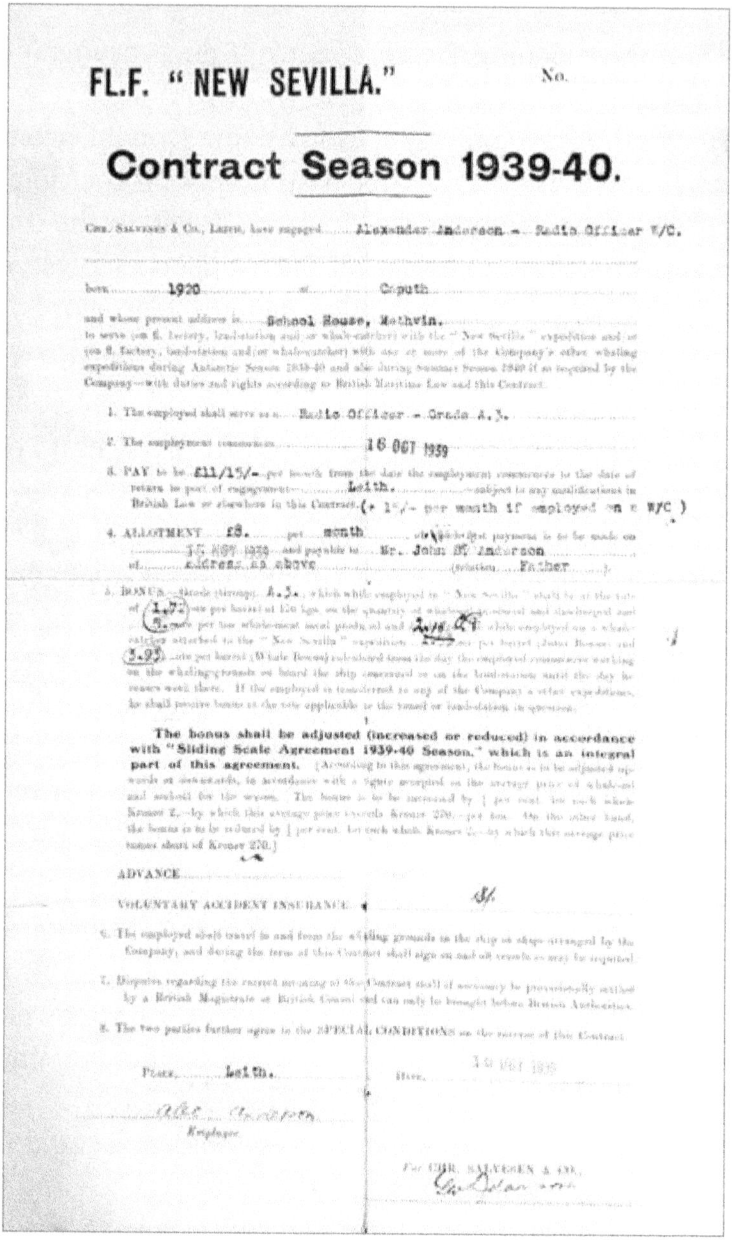

FL.F. " NEW SEVILLA." No.

Contract Season 1939-40.

Chr. Salvesen & Co., Leith, have engaged...... Alexander Anderson — Radio Officer W/C.

born.....1920.....at.....Caputh.

and whose present address is.....School House, Methvin.

to serve (on fl. factory, land-station and /or whale-catcher) with the " New Sevilla " expedition and as (on fl. factory, land-station and/or whalecatcher) with one or more of the Company's other whaling expeditions during Antarctic Season 1939-40 and also during summer Season 1940 if so required by the Company—with duties and rights according to British Maritime Law and this Contract.

1. The employed shall serve as a..... Radio Officer - Grade A.3.

2. The employment commences.....16 OCT 1939

3. PAY to be £11/15/- per month from the date the employment commences to the date of return to port of engagement.....Leith.....subject to any modifications in British Law or elsewhere in this Contract.(+ 1s/- per month if employed on a W/C)

4. ALLOTMENT £3. per month ..... Whereof first payment is to be made on .....15 NOV 1939.....and payable to..... Mr. John M. Anderson..... of.....address as above.....(relation..... Father.....).

5. BONUS —(Scale through)..... A.3. , which while employed in " New Sevilla " shall be at the rate of (1.7.) ore per barrel of 150 kgs. on the quantity of whale-oil produced and shall (legal and ..... .) ore per ton whale-meat meal produced and 2.14.6? while employed as a whale-catcher attached to the " New Sevilla " expedition ..... ore per barrel (Joint Bonus and (5.92) ore per barrel (Whale Bonus) calculated from the day the employed commences working on the whaling-grounds on board the ship concerned or on the land-station until the day he ceases work there. If the employed is transferred to any of the Company's other expeditions, he shall receive bonus at the rate applicable to the vessel or land-station in question.

   The bonus shall be adjusted (increased or reduced) in accordance with "Sliding Scale Agreement 1939-40 Season," which is an integral part of this agreement. [According to this agreement, the bonus is to be adjusted upwards or downwards, in accordance with a figure accepted as the average price of whale-oil and seaboil for the season. The bonus is to be increased by 1 per cent. for each whale Kroner 2,-by which this average price exceeds Kroner 270,- per ton. On the other hand, the bonus is to be reduced by 1 per cent. for each whale Kroner 2,-by which this average price comes short of Kroner 270.]

ADVANCE.....

VOLUNTARY ACCIDENT INSURANCE ..... 3/.

6. The employed shall travel to and from the whaling grounds in the ship or ships arranged by the Company, and during the term of this Contract shall sign on and off vessels as may be required.

7. Disputes regarding the correct meaning of this Contract shall if necessary be provisionally settled by a British Magistrate or British Consul and can only be brought before British Authorities.

8. The two parties further agree to the SPECIAL CONDITIONS on the reverse of this Contract.

Place.....Leith. Date..... 16 OCT 1939

..... Employee

For CHR. SALVESEN & CO.

Fig. 5 - Whaling Expedition Contract

brought the reality that, for the first time in my life, I was on my own.

In the train compartment, I was fortunate in having the company of a seasoned sailor. He had already served on no less than five such expeditions as a 'Donkey-man' (engine-room crew) on-board the 'factory' ship. On our arrival at Newcastle, we transferred to an electric train which took us to Yarrow Buoys Station. This was said to be the most suitable point for reaching the ship. At least, that's what we were told at the office in Leith. It was now 5:30 p.m. and, whereas the train journey thus far had been uneventful, things now began to change. Darkness was falling and there was no taxi to be had. I was, however, fortunate in getting a porter to carry my very heavy case, leaving me with a smaller case and heavy overcoat.

It was a long walk to reach the docks. After searching for some time without any sign of the ship, we were at the point of giving up when a man informed us the ship was not lying in the river at Tyne Dock. It was, in fact, lying some distance down-river. We then had a long trek back to the main road where we were directed onto a bus by my porter and given some further instructions. Dispensing with his services, I gave him a generous tip and my grateful thanks. We left the bus near the gates of Tyne Dock where, after close inspection of our contract papers, the policeman on duty allowed us in. Thus, once again, we set off on foot, but not before the handle of my heavy case broke off, adding further to my difficulties.

By this time, it was almost pitch black and we had to practically feel our way over the railway lines, along quaysides and finally, over gates. I would never again be as exhausted as I was at that time. I don't believe that we would have reached the ship that night had we not encountered a dock railway man carrying a torch. On explaining our destination, he escorted us across yet more railway lines and gates, until finally reaching a quayside off which the Salvestria was lying, a short distance into the river. We then had to hail the ship for the ferryman to row across and transport us back to the ship. It was now 9:30 p.m., which meant that we had spent no less than four hours looking for the ship since leaving Yarrow Buoys Station.

When we finally got on-board, my 'Donkey-man' companion, a Cornishman named Arthur, took me to the room reserved for whale-catcher operators, before going off to find a bunk for himself. The room was situated towards the bow of the ship on the main deck and comprised five pairs of double bunks. Two of the bunks were occupied and I was told their absent occupants were currently onshore. Choosing an empty lower bunk, I deposited my belongings. I was then taken below deck by some friendly chaps for a very welcome mug of tea. Going through the ship for the first time, there was one thing I quickly became very conscious of - a most unpleasant odour. It turned out to be the smell of whale oil, which I soon found out was very difficult to get rid of.

Being dead-beat, I did not linger over my tea and soon returned to my bunk. To say the bunk room was unattractive would be the understatement of the year. It was no surprise to later learn, during the actual fishing period, that it was used to store equipment. Owing to the fact that the Salvestria had to board the crew for all the whale catchers and factory ships as well as her own – totalling more than 350 men – every available space had to be used as accommodation. The situation of the room was something else that I was to regret later, namely when we encountered bad weather.

The room was entirely bare apart from the five double-tiered iron-framed bunks and a maze of large steam pipes criss-crossing the deckhead. The bunks only had a straw palliasse to lie on, and the whole place was crawling with cockroaches. I thought to myself that if the ship had been lying at Leith, rather than South Shields, I would probably have left it. If my father had seen it, he would probably have insisted upon it.

As the officer in charge of the storeroom had gone ashore with the keys, I was unable to get blankets for my bunk. After clearing away the cockroaches, I lay down on top of my raincoat and covered myself with my heavy topcoat. It was some time before I got to sleep because the overhead steam pipes kept hissing, which made the room quite stuffy. I heard the other two radio officers arriving later in the night, but I was too tired to get into conversation. I pretended to be asleep. However, I was conscious of one of them coming up to my case that was lying beside my bunk and, after reading out my name to his companion, said, *"Poor bugger!"* Thus, ended a memorable first day. So much for my horoscope.

I rose at 9 a.m. the next morning and met the other two occupants. They admitted that it was 2 a.m. when they had returned on-board. They were both nice lads. Robertson, the elder of the two, was about thirty-six years old and married. He came from Leith and had been to sea before, both as a seaman and as an operator. Naismith was about twenty-four years old and came from Dalkeith. He had been in the Naval Reserves, but this was his first trip as an operator.

We made our way to the mess room for breakfast and had tea, brown bread and a boiled egg. Porridge was available but I chose not to take any. On returning to our room, I had a wash and shave in a bucket as there were no other facilities available. Robertson and Naismith had decided that they would return to their homes as they had heard a rumour we would not be sailing before Friday. However, they were refused permission to leave.

I changed my bunk today, transferring to another that was nearer to a porthole where I hoped to get some more air. The ship's winches were busy most of the day, taking stores aboard. I also met Captain Jamieson today who wrote out a pass to enable me to get through the Dock gates. He also introduced me to the chief R/O who was, like the captain, a Shetlander. I found them both to be very friendly gentlemen.

I learned from a newspaper report that German planes had been flying over Edinburgh yesterday, dropping bombs close to the Forth Railway Bridge, and I hoped that my father had made it safely across. We also had our first air-raid alarm today. Although the anti-aircraft guns along both banks of our river were clearly manned and ready, we saw no sign of planes. Going ashore with the other lads for the first time, I had my first good look at the ship from the dockside. I was particularly interested in the large opening in the stern, up which whales would be drawn onto the main deck.

There was also a large gun mounted at the stern, which I initially assumed was for defensive purposes. However, I was later told that it was in fact destined for South Georgia, to defend the entrance to Leith Harbour. Having had tea in a café, we decided to go to the cinema, where we saw 'The Oklahoma Kid'. Returning later to Salvestria, we found that MacDonald had arrived (with his kit) from Dundee.

On my third day, I was called to officially sign-on the crew list. I had another chat with the chief R/O who showed me over the radio room, after which I helped him check all the equipment spares. That night, I had my first decent sleep since coming on-board. The following evening, Robertson and I returned to the cinema, whilst Naismith and MacDonald ventured into Newcastle. When the latter pair returned, they produced four Swiss rolls which we proceeded to devour with gusto. There were signs of a stye developing on my right eye and Naismith gave me some ointment to apply to it. Watches commenced tonight and there were rumours that we might sail tomorrow.

It was not to be, and we remained in situ at the dock. On Saturday morning, we found that a former Union Castle Line ship had moored practically alongside us. She was painted grey, having been converted into an Armed Raider. These vessels were well-equipped with searchlights and guns of many types. Departure edged ever closer as a large party of rather unhappy Norwegians arrived on-board from their home country today. They had come across to Lerwick in the Shetland Isles and travelled down the west coast to Liverpool, before heading overland to join the ship on the east coast.

Firstly, they were very angry that their ship had received no escort protection when traversing the southerly west coast route to Liverpool. Secondly, they were made even more unhappy on learning that we were to be sailing south through the English Channel. Apparently, they would have preferred to sail around the north of Scotland. It soon became obvious that they were desperately concerned about the looming war and the latest news of Herr Hitler, who they truly hated. These feelings had naturally become heightened whenever the Germans began sinking Norwegian ships. Once aboard, their concerns were diverted to the fact that there were only six vacant berths in our room, so the rest had to be accommodated elsewhere.

One of the Norwegians, who was perhaps in his mid-thirties, spoke perfect English, albeit with a slight American accent. He had lived in the States for fourteen years, and also served in the US Army for nine of those years. Finally, a lack of work had caused him to return to Norway and he was now going to serve as a steward on a whale catcher. It seemed that the biggest fear in Norway was that they might be invaded by Russia, but they felt sure that America would come to their aid if that happened.

Another of their party was forty-five years old and also spoke excellent English having served in the US Coastguard for many years. He must have been a keep-fit enthusiast as he had an impressive physique. In our relationships with the Norwegians, a curious and, to me, somewhat embarrassing situation became evident. When I was being addressed by one of the Norwegians, they would call me 'Mister Anderson'. This was not the case when they spoke to the other lads. I was later told that the reason for this was that my surname was Swedish in origin and my Christian name (Alex) was also common among Norwegians.

A week after my arrival, the weather had changed for the worse. However, the resultant breeze was very welcome as our room had been like a hothouse. Naismith, MacDonald and I decided to go ashore in the late afternoon, but on reaching the gangway, we were stopped by the fifth mate who said orders had been given that no one was to be allowed ashore. It was Tuesday 24th October when we were allocated our lifeboat stations. A naval gunner also arrived with a WWI Lewis Gun and ammunition which he set up on deck. This was to be our anti-aircraft defence sailing down the coast and through the Channel. It all looked a bit ridiculous compared to what we may be up against.

We cast off at 2:15 p.m. as two tugs took us downriver. Fortunately, I had managed to get to the boatman before leaving and had given him a letter to post home. As we passed the dockyards, we could see many trawlers that were being converted into Minesweepers. On reaching the estuary, we circled around for the purposes of compass adjustments. Having dropped off the pilot, we anchored before joining a passing convoy at 8 p.m. Naismith was going on watch at midnight, having been told that he was to be serving as third R/O.

Waking on the third day, I was aware it had rained all through the previous night. We were now in convoy with a few colliers and there were planes patrolling overhead. I didn't feel too well in the morning and decided not to take any lunch but took a little brandy instead and lay down on my bunk. The other lads said that they too were not feeling so good but at least had managed to eat something. MacDonald was nearly demented because he had no cigarettes left. It appears that most of the British crew members were in the same predicament, but not so the Norwegians. They rolled their own cigarettes and had plenty of shag tobacco available to them.

Naismith returned to the room and told me that I was to take over the midnight to 4 a.m. watch instead of him, so I thought it would be wise to try and get some sleep. The convoy now consisted of ten vessels with an escort of five naval ships, but our progress was slow because of the heavily laden colliers. We were expected to reach Southend by early morning. As I returned to our room, 'Taxi', a messboy came in, so-called because he always wore a peaked cap commonly worn by taxi drivers. With a flourish, he presented MacDonald with a Woodbine cigarette packet. It turned out that it was stuffed full of shag tobacco which he had scrounged from a Norwegian at the tea table. Like a flash, MacDonald became a changed man, immediately filling his pipe with the 'weed' and proceeding to puff away contentedly.

Trying to get to sleep in preparation for the night-time watch was hopeless, what with Taxi joining the other lads in a card game, not to mention the babble from the Norwegians conversing in their own tongue. All this was further added to by the strains of 'Danny Boy' and various Scottish airs coming from an accordion in a neighbouring cabin. At most, I might have had about an hour's fitful sleep by the time I was roused by MacDonald. It was ten minutes to twelve.

I made my way along the main deck and was about to mount the steps to the upper deck when a great gust of wind blew my cap off. Luckily, I managed to retrieve it as it became jammed against a hatch cover before being blown overboard. There was very little doing during my watch, which was just as well, because there was a lot of static interference. I shut down the gear and locked the radio room door before returning to my bunk.

We dropped anchor at 10 a.m. It was a nice day and Southend was a lovely sight. I didn't get up for breakfast as a persistent headache was still troubling me, but I managed to take some lunch. We were lying quite close to the famous pier and there must have been about fifty ships lying around us. Our navy gunner left us today, complete with his gun!

Practically every man you met on deck or in the ship's alleyways asked the same question: *"Have you any cigarettes?"* Apparently, the ship's slop chest did not open for business until the ship was three clear days out to sea and away from land. Naismith told me he was taking the afternoon watch. At 4 p.m., we had a boat drill and were issued with personal books to order from the slop chest. It was a very cold night with strong winds as five searchlights kept watch, sweeping the sky above us.

Following a good night's sleep, despite the activity, we lifted anchor at 8:15 a.m. along with two other ships. One was a French vessel and the other Dutch, and we were also accompanied by two Royal Navy destroyers. As we left the bay, we passed close to the liner, SS Strathallan, where passengers were lining the deck. As soon as I had my first sighting of the white cliffs of Dover, we heard heavy gunfire, but it turned out to be practice shooting at sea targets.

Saturday turned out to be a 'dirty' day with a bad swell running, which meant I was feeling squeamish again. I also seemed to be developing the recurrence of another stye. The ship's slop chest opened today but for the sale of cigarettes only, which did not affect me. I was quickly learning the importance of weather when it comes to sea travel. This fact was well illustrated the same day when Taxi, the messboy, fell down a flight of steps whilst carrying a large dish of stew. Weather aside, on-board chores continued regardless. This was confirmed when Naismith returned to our room with the news that we had to clean all the gear in the radio room.

As we reached the end of the weekend, the weather improved slightly, as did our mood when Taxi arrived on Sunday morning with a tray of buns and pastries. Although not freshly baked, they were, nevertheless, a very welcome treat. I had never been offered anything like this before. Once again, however, fortunes quickly changed when I began feeling squeamish. As a result, I didn't go down for lunch. MacDonald and Robertson were good enough to bring me back an apple and an orange, which I did enjoy.

After tea, Naismith played his accordion, with Taxi and Eddie – the ship's electrician – giving him strong encouragement. Going to the mess room at 8 p.m for supper, we found another accordionist was performing, so he and Naismith joined forces. The rest of the evening was spent playing popular songs, old and new. We returned to our room about half past ten and I was feeling the better of the evening's entertainment, hoping that it would become a regular feature.

After only a few days, our destroyer escorts, which would become a regular feature when it came to our protection, turned back for home. We were now on our own apart from two other merchant ships that were apparently heading in more or less the same direction. Knowing that our escorts were no longer there made for heightened tensions. In fact, later that same afternoon, one of the large steam pipes on-board ship, right outside our door, burst with a loud explosion. We immediately thought we had been torpedoed!

November brought severe gales. These would often spring up in the early hours, making sleep difficult. During the day, I would go below to Eddie's workshop for a chat but would usually end up feeling terribly sick. It was all the worse when there was nothing to 'come up'. When the sea was pretty fierce, especially around evening time, we would be shipping water badly over the fo'c'sle so we had to ensure that our room door, and all the portholes, were kept firmly shut. Needless to say, mistakes were often made. One such evening, Taxi made a surprise appearance to tell us that the messboy quarters had been flooded out and asked if he could lie on our floor. After retrieving his gear, this is what he did, even though he had no palliasse as his had been completely soaked.

Unfortunately, particularly for us first-timers, the bad weather continued for quite a period. Every two to three minutes, a wave would come crashing against the for'ard-facing wall of the room - all being part of a regular cycle of events in such conditions. This would start with the ship firstly, and slowly, leaning over to one side before suddenly plunging downwards. It seemed like it would never stop. When it did, it only paused for a moment before leaning over to the opposite side and soaring to the top once more. At its zenith, it shuddered violently, before the whole cycle began again. It was not at all pleasant.

Unsurprisingly, there were more sleepless nights for me. With doors and portholes closed, the room was particularly warm and stuffy. Taking periodic mouthfuls of water to ease my thirst, I could do nothing else but lay down, all the while listening to the loud crashing of waves against the ship's side, followed by the resultant down-pouring of water onto the deck outside.

After several days of this, I rose one morning at 8 a.m. to find, at last, that the sea was somewhat calmer. I managed to go below deck for a bucket of cold water and had my first wash in four days. It was also the first time that I had felt able to write any notes. At 11:30 a.m., as Naismith was preparing to go on watch in my place, Stewart, the second R/O, came into our room and said that I had to take the watch myself. I was quite taken aback by his instruction, but more so the manner in which he gave it. I had felt ill for days and quite unable to eat anything.

One Friday morning, Tulloch let me go half an hour before the end of my watch, offering to type out the fairly long message that I had received. I was very grateful for that. Whilst on the afternoon watch, Stewart told me that I had to get a bottle from the doctor for my sickness. I did so and commenced treatment that evening. While still on watch, Captain Jamieson came into the radio room and asked how I was feeling. His parting words were,

"You will soon get over it".

During the midnight to 4 a.m. watch, I received two messages which had to be typed out. Because of the layout of the room, this could only be done whilst standing. I felt so dizzy and weak when standing that I could only manage to do a little at a time, then sit down in between. Later, I managed to take a little breakfast and some lunch, feeling slightly the better for it. However, whilst on the afternoon watch, I began to feel bad. The sea, yet again, had become rough. When I came off watch at 4 p.m., I met the doctor at the door of the saloon. When he asked me how I was feeling, I could only reply, ever-hopefully,

"A little better".

The past week was one which I would never forget and hoped never to experience again. I prayed that, when I began my watch at midnight, my improvement would continue. I hoped by the end of that week to be completely recovered. I must say that all of my companions were most considerate and sympathetic to my plight, particularly Arthur, the Cornish donkey-man who continued to prove himself a true friend.

I was soon able to take some lunch before taking the afternoon watch. Tea (referring to our main meal of the day) could be quite a random selection such as corned beef along with sardines. Strangely, I remember feeling that I could have eaten more, but given recent memory, I decided not to chance my luck. Although usually very sleepy at the beginning of a watch, I managed to get through the following four hours without any problem. For a start, there would always be the opportunity to catch up on the BBC news headlines. In my diary for 5th November 1939, I recorded the following news stories: *'Repeal of Arms in USA', 'SS City of Flint German crew interned in Norway'* and *'Mussolini talks with war chiefs'*.

Days later, I found myself making another diary entry during my watch after hearing an 'SSS' (submarine sighting) distress call. This signified that a ship within our range had either been attacked by a submarine or, at the very least, had sighted one on the surface. Unfortunately, the signal was dreadfully weak and it was not possible either to get the name of the ship or its position, so it must have been a considerable distance away, and at the limit of our range.

One of the ships that had initially set out with us became the subject of a call received by Stewart, the second R/O. He heard an SSS message broadcast from the SS San Jose, stating they were being pursued by a submarine. As Stewart did not hear any acknowledgement of the message from any other ship or a shore station, he re-transmitted the distress call. This would become a regular occurrence as ships would attempt to relay messages to both inform as well as to reach those in a position to provide assistance. Rarely, however, would we ever hear any update or result of messages like this. We would become aware if there was a subsequent news report mentioning the particular ship, or if it was part of a larger, newsworthy event. In due course, I would have some examples when this did in fact happen.

I was soon reminded how some things at sea had remained unchanged for centuries, and this was brought to my notice when we received our first issue of lime juice since leaving land, an ancient remedy to ward off scurvy.

Coming off afternoon watch, I would often unwind by standing out on deck. Sometimes this would coincide with watching flying fish skimming over the waves like swallows. Their silvery bodies would glisten in the bright sunlight when we were lucky enough to enjoy such weather. Once, when I found that one had landed on deck, I was surprised to find that it was only seven to eight inches long.

Ship's crew would very often have multiple tasks and some took on additional functions relative to any additional skills they already had or had acquired through necessity. MacDonald, Naismith and I were regular customers in having our hair cut by one of the firemen onboard. This was a source of extra income, though usually settled by bartering. In this case, payment was made in cigarettes. Other activities also attempted to make up for being away from home. Use of radio sets outside the ship's radio room was forbidden. However, for a bit of fun, some of the crew would make up their own stories as news bulletins, albeit all taken from the realms of fantasy. This situation continued during most of the trip until we were instructed to only put *'worthwhile'* news bulletins on the notice boards.

Once again, the weather was improving, allowing us to enjoy some fine days. However, even after a night of fierce rain, the increasing temperatures meant everyone was now running with sweat. U-boat activity was also heating up. In fact, the chief intercepted a distress message from the factory ship SS Tafelberg. It reported being chased by a submarine only 200-250 miles to the north of our position. The Tafelberg was a South African ship *en route* from Norway, and also heading south to the whaling grounds.

It was a Saturday around mid-November when we passed a chain of islands in the distance, their mountain peaks clearly standing out against the horizon. The warm evenings now allowed some alfresco entertainment. After tea, two accordionists sat out on the hatch outside our room and having attracted a large audience, we had music and singing for the rest of the evening. I recall some lovely nights with a soft warm breeze, and the sky lit up with wildfire. I could not imagine what it would be like without the ever-present sea breeze. Even though I did not feel exceptionally warm, the sweat poured from my body.

As we were expecting to arrive at the island of Aruba in the Dutch West Indies, I finished writing a letter home and posted it in the box provided aboard ship. My excitement at the thought of stepping ashore on a foreign land for the first time in my life was dealt a blow. Stuart, the second R/O, told me that, whilst in port, I had to clean, grease and top-up the radio equipment batteries as well as cleaning and greasing the generators. Stuart was by no means a likeable man at any time, with never the slightest of smiles on his face. And, he was particularly unpleasant to me, for some unknown reason. Mr Tulloch, on the other hand, was completely different.

I thought Stuart was overdoing it by ordering me to carry out this work completely on my own. After all, there were at least three others on-board who, like me, were engaged as radio officers to serve on whale catchers. They, unlike me, were taking no watches on the trip down to South Georgia. It was not as if I was getting paid extra for taking watches on Salvestria. I decided to casually mention the matter to Mr Tulloch when I took over from him at midnight. He replied,

"Just forget it", adding,

"It can easily be done another day".

I would later learn that Stuart had previously served at sea but had left to run a pub in the south of England before the war. However, he was forced to return and 'serve his country'. He certainly was not a happy man. In contrast, and an example of Mr Tulloch's sense of humour, it is worth telling of an incident that had happened only a few days earlier. To reach the radio room, one had to climb stairs close by the saloon, which at night, was mainly occupied by a group of gunners talking and playing cards. When I took up my watch at midnight, there were very audible signs of conviviality and laughter emanating from the saloon, as was the case on many occasions.

On coming off watch at 4 a.m., there would frequently be a row of empty Bols gin bottles, in their distinctive stoneware, sitting outside the saloon door. On the night in question, I relieved Mr Tulloch at midnight. On leaving, he turned at the door and said,

"Oh! I forgot something. Give me a card with the heavy fuse wire and I will return it later".

About half an hour later, the door burst open and there was a shout of,

"Taa-raaah!"

On turning round in my chair, I could not contain myself at the vision confronting me. After my initial hesitation and disbelief, there stood Tulloch in his bare feet, a walking staff in his right hand and clothed, as far as I could see, only in a white bedsheet. To complete his 'outfit', he was wearing the veritable trademark of Mahatma Gandhi – a pair of round spectacle frames, these, of course, having been skilfully fashioned from the (borrowed) fuse wire. It could have been the great man himself.

Trying to suppress my laughter as best I could, I waited outside the radio room until, at Tulloch's hand, the saloon door was thrown open with a flourish and an unintelligible greeting made to the astonished assembly of gunners. A tremendous eruption of laughter rose from the saloon, which only started me off again as I slumped back into my chair. It certainly made my day and, I am sure, the gunners' also.

On coming off the afternoon watch one day, I saw a large crowd standing on the afterdeck and, going to investigate, I found that Taxi was engaged in a wrestling match with 'Pig Boy'. The latter was in charge of a replacement consignment of pigs destined for Leith Harbour, which were housed on the afterdeck. The match ended with the complete exhaustion of both contestants, although I thought that Taxi had come off worst. They were both in some mess, as could be imagined considering their surroundings. The legs of Pig Boy's trousers were so badly torn that there was a temporary halt during the contest. This was to allow both trouser legs to be cut off at the knee using the knife of one of the spectators.

By the end of the contest, the remainder of his overalls were split right up to the waistline. After the open-deck entertainment, there was a queue at the doctor's surgery, where all attendees wanted lotion for sunburnt skin. Although not suffering from sunburn myself, my ankles were quite swollen from the heat alone.

My first sighting of Aruba came at 7:30 a.m. on the 13th of November. What first struck the eye was the sight of many large white oil storage tanks, looking for all the world like very large mushrooms. We berthed at 10 a.m. having been preceded by our sister ship, SS Sourabaya, aboard which, unknown to me at that time, I would later serve. We began taking on oil almost immediately and received our passes for going ashore shortly before midday. I felt quite excited as I stepped onto foreign soil for the first time since the name 'Dutch West Indies' had always held a fascination for me. However, any romantic notions lingering from my youth were not long in being somewhat diluted.

As we walked ashore, we were amazed at the enormous number of oil storage tanks and chimneys, which gave the impression of a continuing series of gas works. Small electric trucks ran at a fair speed on lines between the tanks, and the town was swarming with cars and lorries of the most modern types, all being of American manufacture, such as Ford, Chrysler, Dodge and Plymouth. The population was almost entirely native and although the common language is English, they did converse with each other in their own tongue. Our first stop on getting outside the dock area was at a small wooden shed. Some local men there were pressing gents' suits, apparently operating a dry-cleaning business. However, we were soon made aware there was a quite different type of 'business' being actively operated at the same time.

Crews on whaling ships were not allowed an issue of money at Aruba. Apart from the fact that alcoholic drink was not supposed to be allowed on-board, there was always the risk of men drinking too much whilst ashore, the result being the real risk of failing to return on-board before the ship sailed. Crew members who had been on previous expeditions were all prepared to make use of the alternative 'business' operation by bartering goods for cash. The biggest demand, and most profitable exchange, was for wrist watches, cigarettes and fountain pens. The crew 'old-timers' had prepared in advance by making appropriate purchases, at the earliest opportunity, from Salvestria's slop chest.

Except for the main street where the majority of shops were situated, the streets in Aruba were very narrow. The locals lived in the surrounding streets in what can best be described as shacks. They seemed, at least from the outside, to be dreadful affairs, constructed mainly from old sheets of corrugated iron and parts of packing cases. They looked to be simply thrown together. The shops were constructed mainly of wood, although some of the newer ones were concrete. In most cases, the entire shop front was open to the street, whilst the others had at least two entrance doors. The shopkeepers were of varied ethnicity, including Dutch, Chinese, Mexican and Jewish.

The only one who would accept British silver coins was the Jewish proprietor of the 'Union Stores'. The others would only accept paper money, preferably American or Dutch. There appeared to be no shortage of goods for sale, including refrigerators, washing machines and other electrical appliances. I returned on-board for tea, having made no purchases and did not go ashore again that night.

Fig.6 Author ashore in Aruba, Curacao

The work of taking on oil goes on twenty-four hours a day. In the darkness, it was a great sight to see the whole area of the plant lit up by thousands of lights. They said that there was going to be a trial blackout on 10th December. It would be some undertaking.

Going ashore again, this time with Robertson, we had a walk around and came across one or two nicer houses with gardens. They had small trees and shrubs bearing lovely red and purple flowers which contrasted with the scrub and cactus which abounded elsewhere. We came across some Dutch policemen. They were dressed in a green velvet-like uniform with breeches and leggings and were equipped with a sword, two revolvers and a large ammunition belt.

The naval marines who patrolled within the dock area wore an all-white uniform, carried a rifle with fixed bayonet, and one revolver. On our way back to the dock, I parted with the last of my money, buying a local one-sheet newspaper for three cents and a tub of ice-cream for 25 cents. The former purchase informed me that Holland had been made aware that peace was 'impossible', however, in contrast, the latter provided a great deal of satisfaction. Before boarding the ship, we stood at the dockside watching a large number of lizards that infested the area and marvelled at their agility.

We found that our sister ship, Sourabaya, had sailed in our absence and was replaced at the dock by the Tafelberg, the same ship that we heard of earlier being pursued by an enemy submarine. That same afternoon, I was walking along the after-lifeboat deck, and, on passing one of the boats, was suddenly aware of an overwhelming sickly, scented smell. I could not understand where it was coming from until I stooped to look under the boat. There, sprawled out, lay a Norwegian, an empty 'Brilliantine' bottle still clutched in his hand. He had obviously consumed the perfumed hair product contents and was 'dead to the world', however, I did not linger as I felt quite nauseated by the fumes.

We sailed out in the evening about 8 p.m. and I commenced my watch again at midnight. On my way to the radio room, I noticed a group of messboys standing at the door to the ship's hospital. On mentioning this to Tulloch, he told me that they had come to him earlier saying that one of their mates had gone to sleep in the afternoon and they could not wake him. Going down to see if he could do anything, he too was unable to rouse him, so he told the boys to call the doctor.

Later into my watch, the captain arrived and handed me the estimated list of approximate positions of the ship over the next four hours. Enquiring as to the messboy incident, he said that over-exposure to heat had caused his condition. The captain had apparently come across a similar case before but was surprised that the doctor had not! However, a few days later, the messboy was making a good recovery.

With regard to the captain's list of the ship's positions, these were given to the bridge at the beginning of every four-hour watch indicating our estimated position at each consecutive hour. The reason for this was that, in the event of anything serious happening, the R/O on duty could immediately send out a distress message giving our relevant position at that time.

Radio transmission from ships was not allowed except in cases of distress and the normal 'SOS' prefix had to be substituted by a coded prefix which indicated the nature of the attack, whether by submarine, surface ship or by aircraft. It was only by special permission of the Government that radio transmission was being allowed at the whaling grounds subject to certain limitations. But, of course, radio contact between the catchers and their factory ship was an essential requirement for the whole operation.

I heard today, unsurprisingly, that there was an acute shortage of clocks and watches on-board - the result of bartering for local currency in Aruba. The good news is that I had now earned my first month's pay, although it would be some time before I actually saw any of it. It was raining heavily when I took up my watch at midnight, but it turned out to be a grand day despite a strong wind blowing which resulted in our taking on a lot of sea-spray.

Work was now in full swing on deck. A protective wooden floor was being laid over the ship's deck to protect it from damage during the cutting-up of the whales. The wind made it a great deal cooler today and my ankles, which had been swollen and giving me some bother lately, now felt a lot better. When Stuart arrived to commence his watch at 4 p.m., he delighted in informing me,

"I've got a job for you tomorrow; come up after breakfast".

My brain immediately made some calculations. Breakfast, at the latest, was 8 a.m. and, as I would not get to my bunk until 4:30 p.m., I wondered when he thought I would be likely to get some sleep. In addition, I would need to get washed and get down for lunch by 11:30 a.m., all prior to going on watch again at midday. However, I decided to say nothing, at least for the time being.

When Stuart eventually relieved me just after 4 a.m. (he was often prone to being late when taking over from my watch), he gruffly reminded me of what he had said the previous afternoon. Looking for a compromise, I replied,

"Would the afternoon do?"

"No, it won't!", was his immediate answer, followed by,

"Anyway, you are on watch!"

I countered this by saying that I meant after my watch was finished which would allow me to get some sleep in the forenoon. This was apparently the 'last straw' for Mr Stuart. Going completely off the deep end, he screamed back at me,

"What a bloody cheek!" He continued,

"When I was at sea before the war, I used to work 14 hours a day…".

I turned about in retreat and walked away without another word, leaving him standing there, still raving. On coming up from breakfast, I met Naismith who told me that Stuart had stopped him and asked where I was, and when told, replied,

"TELL HIM TO COME UP NOW!"

It was about nine o'clock when I got upstairs to do the job, which, I had learned by this time, was to check, clean and top-up the acid batteries. I expected that I might be able to complete the job in one go, or at the most, by taking another morning to finish. However, surprise, surprise! Mr Stuart must have had a rare bout of conscience. He completely surprised me on my arrival by reducing my task to topping up only two of the small six-volt batteries. Despite my protestations that I would prefer to go ahead and do as much as possible, he would not hear of it. He left muttering something about wanting the other batteries on charge.

I awoke on Saturday with a bad headache. When I arrived to continue the job on the batteries, I was greeted by Stuart with a customary sarcastic remark:

"Oh, so there you are! ... I'm nearly finished".

I found that he had done two of the large six-volt batteries, leaving me to do the remaining four and re-assemble the lot in their container. When I had finished and washed, I took two aspirins and lay on my bunk for three-quarters of an hour before going down for lunch.

However, I could not eat much, but my head did get easier during the course of the afternoon watch.

This was the end of another week and I found that time was passing more quickly now. Since leaving Aruba, the weather had become much cooler due to the breeze that was blowing, and I was not sweating to the same extent. I hoped this would continue till we 'crossed the line', which would not be long now. It was still pretty close at night, and although the sea was quite calm, we were taking quite a lot of spray over the bow due to us sailing much lower in the sea with the large amount of oil we had taken on board in Aruba. However, to round off the day, we were treated to a beautiful sunset.

After tea on Sunday, I visited Eddie's room with some of the lads, but left at half past seven to get some sleep before going on watch at midnight. Before leaving, however, I was fortunate to hear Eddie tell a very funny story, which he swore was completely true. The incident in question had taken place on a previous voyage to the whaling grounds. One morning, the second mate on the factory ship mentioned to the second engineer that he needed a bolt and nut to fix something on deck, but he was not sure about the size he required.

"That's alright", the engineer replied, *"I will send one of the firemen up with a box of assorted sizes, and you can pick out what you need."*

When the fireman duly arrived, the mate soon found the right size of bolt and then said to the fireman,

"Now, if we can only find the right nut to fit."

Eager to help, the fireman triumphantly picked out a nut he believed would fit and handed it over. However, the mate found that it was no use, having a different type of thread, and unceremoniously threw it back into the box. The fireman, a Norwegian and not very fluent in English, was clearly upset at the mate's dismissive action and, offering up his hands in surprise, asked,

"What wrong with it?"

Suddenly, the mate replied,

"Odd bastard!"

There was an immediate uproar from the fireman who leapt at the mate, grabbing him by the throat and screaming,

"You no say that; no true, no true!"

Peace was eventually restored when an onlooker intervened and explained to the mate that the second engineer who sent up the fireman with the box was named 'Aad' which, in Norwegian, was pronounced 'Odd'!

At the beginning of the new week, I was surprised to find out there had been an outbreak of mumps on-board. I was not sure if there was any significance in this, although it seemed to coincide with talk between some of the crew members becoming more and more heated. It had become a habit lately for four of us to sit out on deck after tea, but unfortunately, talk became more and more politically inclined.

A couple in our group seemed very aggressive in their beliefs, such as, *'Britain should give up all her colonies and keep to herself'* and *'Germany should be given all her demands'*. The list continued with Scottish and Irish nationalism, and antisemitism, not to mention conspiracy theories that the reported dumping of mines in the North Sea had just as likely been done by Britain. The latter claim, namely risking the sinking of our own ships, was, in their minds, solely to get sympathy from neutral countries by blaming it on Germany. I simply failed to understand them. I realised I must avoid being drawn into these discussions in the future.

We crossed the line on Thursday 23rd November at 6 a.m. The day turned out to be like a good summer's day back at home, but without the roasting heat that I, in my innocence, had expected on my first crossing of the equator. Another surprise today was to see that the sea around us was completely brown in colour. This prompted a visit to the bridge where the mate informed me that this was the outflow from the Amazon. With no land in sight, this impressed upon me the sheer magnitude of that mighty river.

During my early morning watch on the following Monday, I listened to a speech by Prime Minister Chamberlain, which he ended with the words,

"Then let us go forward with God's blessing in our hands, and we shall prevail."

It was also reported today that the SS Rawalpindi had been sunk by enemy action. I later heard some details of the sinking of the Rawalpindi, which had taken place off the coast of Iceland. It was reported that the bridge and radio room were completely shot away by the fourth salvo of fire, and that thirty survivors had been picked up by the Germans and a further eleven by the ship SS Chitral. The remainder of the crew were presumed to have perished.

This was the warmest day since leaving Aruba, probably due to the fact that the previously persistent breeze had dropped. After tea, there was some concerned excitement on deck. Something was seen cutting the surface of the sea on the port side, leaving a white wash in its wake. However, it turned out to be a large fish and not, as I believe some feared, a submarine periscope. The moon was full now and it was a magnificent sight to witness it rising on the horizon, and its rays gradually spreading out over the sea.

I finished cleaning the radio room batteries this morning, and afterwards, lay out in the sun and got sunburned in the process. During the afternoon, there was a sudden change in the weather when the sky became overcast and heavy rain followed. During the evening, I made my first purchases from the slop chest, including a packet of 200 Lucky Strike American cigarettes. I intended having my hair cut and it is usual to give the barber some cigarettes. The slop chest had been sold out of chocolate and sweets for some weeks now and this had resulted in my taking the occasional cigarette, which I feared may become a bad habit.

I witnessed a mass slaughter of cockroaches during my afternoon watch, when Tulloch arrived with a Flit spray, which he directed into all the corners. The 'beasts' came out in their scores, but on being sprayed again, they promptly succumbed. When I returned on watch at midnight, Tulloch was still on the attack. During my four-hour stint, I followed suit, as there were a few still scuttling about.

The last day of November rewarded me with the sight of my first albatross. It had a tremendous wingspan which seemed to be out of proportion to its body and it swooped over the waves with no apparent movement of its wings. The engineers had been passing steam through the oil tanks so that the contents would be more easily pumped-out when we reached Leith Harbour on South Georgia, hopefully in a week's time. I heard on the news today that Russia had invaded Finland.

As we entered December, it was clear that we were definitely out of the tropics now and shipping a lot of water over the bows in heavy swells. This continued into the following day when we shipped water continuously. The ship was tossing and rolling badly, with many cabins being flooded out as a result. I was fortunate in having the only dry bunk at the end of the day.

We reached forty degrees south during the afternoon and there was a strange, heavy feeling in the air. I had been taking a watch for one month now and it was noticeable that the hours of darkness were now reduced. Although it was pitch dark when I went on watch at midnight, it was clear daylight when I finished at 4 a.m. Naismith, MacDonald and I had our hair cut by one of the Norwegian crew. We expect to reach South Georgia in two days or so.

When I arrived to take over my early morning watch, I was quite surprised when Tulloch asked me to go down to the galley for two cups of tea and toast, or fried bread. I found out that there was no butter but I was able to fry two slices of bread and return triumphantly to the radio room. I was already regretting the fact that I had not been previously aware of this facility before or after my night watch.

On coming off my afternoon watch at four o'clock, Tulloch told me not to bother coming on watch at midnight, as we were expecting to reach the island early next morning. This suited me as I would have plenty of time to write a letter home and pack my case to move ship. Having been transported to the South Atlantic, the real adventure was now about to begin.

I got to bed shortly after midnight and awakened at 4a.m. I had specifically asked MacDonald to call me when we were approaching South Georgia, however, he had either slept in or had forgotten my request. On being informed that we were already lying at anchor in Leith Harbour, I decided to roll over and lie there for another two hours before rising. Once awake, and meeting Naismith on deck, we were rewarded with a most wonderful vista.

It was 6th December 1939, and we were lying in a beautiful natural harbour. On our port side lay the narrow entrance channel. On each side, and stretching round the harbour, snow-covered mountains rose majestically from near to the water's edge. Close to the shore lay the catchers, their 'mother' ships and other vessels. It was a magnificent sight.

Fig.7 Leith Harbour, South Georgia

Both MacDonald and I were contracted to the New Sevilla expedition so, complete with kit, we took the motor launch ashore to sign-on. I was informed I was to serve on the whale catcher, MV Sirra.

Chapter 2 – MV Sirra

Fig.8 MV Sirra with whale alongside

When I finally located Sirra, she was tied up with other catchers, but I found her deserted. The equipment in the radio room was not yet fully assembled, neither were there any stores on-board, nor any heating or lighting. Nevertheless, I retired to my bunk and, covered by my great coat, spent a very cold night in the shadow of the snow-covered mountains.

I have no idea when I eventually got to sleep during the night but come it did. I must have been sound because on wakening the next day, I discovered to my surprise that we were now alongside the Sevilla. Later on shore, I met MacDonald carrying a box which he informed me contained all the necessary spares for the radio room on the catcher and had to be collected from a building on shore. After uplifting the appropriate box, I returned to Sirra, but on checking the equipment, I found that the aerial was broken and the radio receiver was not working.

To cap it all, I learned that the chief R/O on the Sevilla was expected to come on-board tomorrow to inspect all the gear. To add insult to injury, I had developed a very large swelling on my neck behind my right ear. It was arising from a boil which the doctor on Salvestria had lanced on Monday, but it was much worse now. If it did not improve soon, I would try to see the doctor on Sevilla.

On Friday, I got one of the crew to fix the aerial, and, with Robertson's aid, carried aboard a nice GEC radio receiver. This was being supplied to catchers that didn't have radiotelephone transmitter/receivers. This enabled us to listen in to catchers that did have the radiotelephone facility. In the afternoon, we were preparing to leave for a small settlement a short distance away to take on a supply of fresh water, when I was told that I had to go aboard Sevilla to collect a copy of the codes which were to be used during the fishing period. Each expedition had its own set of codes in order to prevent other whalers from knowing where, or if, it was seeing plentiful numbers of fish, and thus protecting its own catches.

It was a bit of a shock to find that the codes were all in Norwegian and without any English translation, but there was no time for receiving explanations, as I had to rush back on board Sirra. On arrival there, I found the radio officer in charge of Shore Operations waiting for me. He had been trying to repair the main radio receiver, but because of our imminent departure, was unable to do so in the time available. His name was Hawick and he came from Shetland. He had not returned home at the end of the previous season but had stayed on, or 'over-wintered', as it was commonly referred to. I learned later that Mr Hawick also acted as the dentist on the island, performing extractions of troublesome molars.

Our destination for fresh water was named Stromness, a small-scale, shore-based whaling station operated there. When we arrived, I could see a colony of sea lions lying on the shore beside a small burn flowing into the sea. Others were often seen at Leith Harbour alongside penguins and king penguins. One domesticated animal that was invariably encountered along the harbour-front was a poor goat, which seemed to have a nicotine craving, judging by the number of cigarettes it was seen to consume!

Like a duck with its new brood, the New Sevilla sailed out of Leith Harbour that evening with her six catchers, including the Sirra, following close behind. I had been told many frightening stories about the dreadful tossing and shaking that one would experience on a catcher. So, on leaving the harbour, I was quite relieved to find that, at least so far, the sea was very calm. However, the big unknown lay ahead and would last for the next three months.

Before going to my bunk last night, I was, thankfully, able to repair the previously non-functioning main radio receiver. It was a bonus to discover that the GEC radio was a grand set for receiving news from home. At 7:30 a.m., the steward wakened me for breakfast. Meals were taken in a small mess room adjoining the steward's kitchen which was situated amidships. This was shared by the gunner (who was also master of the ship), the mate, two engineers and myself.

My companions were Norwegians and all, including the steward, were able to speak English. As it turned out, they were very good to me and most considerate. After breakfast, I returned to my cabin to listen to the factory ship. I was relieved when I heard her making test signals, thus confirming that my repairs had, indeed, been successful. The sea was still calm and small blocks of ice could be seen floating on the surface.

My combined radio room and cabin was situated on the lifeboat deck close to the stern. Access was from the main deck by a ladder to the entrance door which faced aft. I never did manage to accurately measure the size of the room, but it certainly could not have been greater than ten feet by eight feet. Thankfully, the door opened outwards, which helped a little. My desk, which held the radio equipment, stood against the forward-facing wall and slightly L-shaped round the port side. The porthole above the desk looked out to the bridge and funnel and was the only natural light source. My bunk was against the starboard wall, with the top end resting on my desk. On the port side were a small, fixed seat and wash-hand basin. A desk chair completed the contents of my room.

Sunday 10th December 1939 was the big day when we received orders to commence fishing. This marked the first day of the three-month-long 1939-40 season. It was not long before we came on several whales. I must admit to having been quite excited back then to be on the bridge to see our first catch. However, it was not a good start for us, particularly for the gunner, as our total catch for the day was a disappointing... zero!

Fig.9 MV Sirra Harpoon Gunner

I suppose there was some excuse for the poor gunner, as it was nine months since he had last used the gun. He was on target on two occasions but unfortunately, the harpoon ricocheted off his quarry. The gunner was never very popular with the crew when a miss was recorded. The more whales that were caught, the bigger their bonus was at the end of the season.

Also, a good part of fishing time was wasted when a miss occurred as the line had to be retrieved, recoiled, refitted to a new harpoon and, finally, loaded back into the gun. We chased one whale along by the side of a lovely iceberg, some parts of which were bright blue in colour and some others, near to the water line, were green. Our chase led us into pack ice where we lost sight of our quarry, but I was interested to have my first sightings of penguins at close quarters in the open sea and jumping from floe to floe.

Next day, we sighted a large school of blue whales, which are the largest and most sought-after type. I sent a message to the factory ship giving them details including our present location. We were unable to make up on them, however, but later in the day, we did encounter another blue. As we made up on it, the gunner quickly descended the catwalk from the bridge towards the gun which was mounted on the bow.

As we closed in, he gave directions with his hands as to which way he wanted the wheelman to steer the ship. The gunner had the best viewing position to see the dull shape of the whale through the clear water as it came up to the surface to blow. When the range was believed right, the gunner held up his hand in a 'steady' signal, and when the arched back presented itself, he fired. This time, it was a direct hit and we were 'fast', as it was called, to our first fish.

However, it was not a vital hit, and the whale put up a terrific fight. We had to chase after it, reeling in as best we could and, once within firing distance again, another harpoon was fired, this time without a line. Unfortunately, this did not prove to be the *coup de grace* that was intended. When it was below the surface, its position remained known as flocks of sea-birds followed its progress and would swoop down on the water. Eventually, it was necessary to fire a third to put it out of its misery and finally complete the task.

When the carcase was brought alongside, a metal pipe with holes, like an outsized gas poker, was inserted into the body. This allowed compressed air to be pumped in which enabled it to float and be more easily towed into the factory ship. I contacted the factory to notify them of our catch and that we were returning right away as our fuel tanks required replenishing. Thus, we set off with the whale lying alongside us, its tail being secured by means of a noose to a bollard near to our bow, whilst the head was streaming out towards our stern.

We reached the factory at 9 p.m. and found that work on-board was in full swing. We were pleased to learn later that our first whale, at eighty feet in length, was the largest caught so far. A rough measure of the weight is to allow one ton for every foot, thus at eighty tons, was only eight tons short of Sirra's own net weight. After transferring the whale, we moved alongside to get our fuel tanks filled. I took the opportunity to climb the rope ladder to the factory, firstly to hand in lists for the crew for their slop chest requirements, and secondly, to see the doctor about my swollen neck. He gave me an injection and lanced and dressed the infected swelling. He gave me a supply of lint and bandages, with instructions to have it dressed twice daily by the mate.

Fig.10 Factory Ship with whales on stern slipway

Work goes on twenty-four hours a day on the factory with huge floodlights shining on deck. It is a noisy, active scene with shouting, the rattling of winches, the screaming of bone saws and the hissing of steam. Whenever a whale is drawn up on deck through the slipway at the stern, the

Flensers, as they are called, get to work on the carcase, some from the side and with others standing on top of it. With long-handled wooden blades, for all the world similar to very large hockey sticks, and aided by winches, they strip off the blubber and cut up the meat.

This is cut into pieces and dropped into the boilers below deck. The bones are cut up by saws and also dropped below decks, where they are made into bonemeal. The entire operation, as can be imagined, is a very messy and unpleasant job. It was about 11 p.m. before we left the factory, and after spending some time adjusting my transmitter, I finally got to my bunk at 1 a.m.

The next day again was very cold, and, after listening in to the factory, I put on my heavy coat and muffler before going up to the bridge around 8:30 a.m. Between nine and ten o'clock, we sighted a blue and began chasing, but lost sight of it several times as it moved into pack ice, which was pretty solid. This resulted in our having to circle around, which allowed the blue to swim under the ice. Several seals were lying on the ice and, despite us sometimes brushing against the floes, they didn't seem too bothered. Some of them even carried on dozing. We finally got within range of our target at about 11:15 a.m. Thankfully, it succumbed with the first shot, despite being even larger than yesterday's catch.

As there were no other fish in sight, we returned to the factory. Soon after dropping off the blue, another was sighted and it also led us into more pack ice. Once again, our gunner made a direct hit but the whale put up a great fight. I missed most of the action being on radio watch at the time, only getting an occasional glimpse through my cabin's solitary porthole.

On one occasion, the whale was lashing about with its gigantic tail threshing the sea. It seemed that it was trying to throw itself onto the ice. When the whale was finally secured with the aid of a further harpoon, the tail was fastened to the port bow as usual. However, it so happened that the body ended up lying directly across our bows. I was greatly intrigued to see how this was going to be corrected. The ship reduced speed to 'slow-ahead' until the body was against a fairly large ice floe. By turning to port, with the pressure between our starboard side and the ice, the whale was forced under the ship to take up the preferred position on the port side. During this operation, the ship took on an alarming list, and I was glad that I was not up in the crow's nest at the time.

On retracing our path through the ice, we came upon large colonies of penguins. They were very amusing to watch as they chattered whilst jumping on and off the floes. As for the seals, they did not bother themselves at all, unless we happened to come very close against the ice. Unlike the penguins, they did not give us much in the way of entertainment. In a vain attempt to rectify that situation, I have to make an admission. On occasion, I would throw a few potatoes at them, firstly making sure that the steward was not around. The box in which the potatoes were kept was situated at the stern below my cabin. Unfortunately, this made them temptingly close, as a later incident will tell.

At eight in the evening, whilst still on our way back, I received a message from the factory instructing us to stop fishing and return, as they currently had too many whales to handle. On our arrival, and because of this situation, we had to stand-by the factory whilst still retaining our catch. Going out on deck next morning, I found that we were holding a further three whales. These had been brought in during the night by two of the other catchers.

The reason for our being called in to assist in this way was that Sirra had been designated as the Buoy Boat for the expedition and could be called upon at any time to carry out various tasks as required. These could include such duties as searching given areas for signs of whales when catches were low, and the transporting back to South Georgia of seriously ill or injured crew.

Acting as the Buoy Boat could be financially beneficial to its crew. Our catch bonus would be determined by the average catch of all the boats at the end of the season. However, the bonus for the others depended on their individual catch alone. I was relieved when the factory took all the whales over from us at midday, as they were beginning to smell, however, fortunately, no incisions had yet been made in the carcases. These would require to be done when the carcase swelled up in order to let the accumulating gases escape. Otherwise, the quality of the extracted oil was impaired. This task was carried out by the mate with the use of a flensing knife, and after two days waiting time, the resultant smell is frankly indescribable!

Shortly after setting off once again, and still in sight of the factory, we came upon a fish which was caught very quickly and turned out to be a whale. On getting it alongside, we intended heading back to hand it in, when we came upon a big blue. Releasing the whale with one of our flags attached to show ownership, we continued the chase. This blue was a very large fish. On being harpooned, it set off strongly towards pack ice and duly disappeared underneath. The ship, on the other hand, had to force its way through. Fortunately, the floes were not large and, after getting through, we soon secured our second catch.

On returning to retrieve our floating fin, another of the same species was sighted so the blue was also dropped, and another chase swiftly followed. Our first shot was a hit, but not vital. As the line was being drawn in to facilitate the firing of another shot, there was a sudden jerk. Before the strain on the rope could be released, there was a loud 'crack' as it parted. Fortunately, we were able to catch up with our quarry and successfully complete the capture at about 10 p.m. After retrieving our other two fish, we returned to the factory and handed over the trio in the early hours of the following morning.

After that long day, and despite having been wakened as usual by the steward, I slept in next morning. We saw some whales during the day but they were considered too small to comply with the strict international regulations. It would be night before we made our only catch of the day. However, it was a large fish and was being winched in, presumed dead. Then, only thirty feet or so away, and lying on the surface, it suddenly came to life to charge our starboard side. It hit us head-on before it disappeared right under the ship to the other side. This gave us more than just a little concern that we might be in some trouble.

Fortunately for us, this had proved to be a last dying struggle, and it was soon over. We had intended flagging this whale as we had done yesterday, to chase another, but fog was coming down. Rather than risk losing the flagged fish in the fog, we returned to the factory. Our progress was slow because of the fog and I was constantly on watch, taking regular radio bearings from the factory until we finally arrived back at 3:30 a.m. It was mid-forenoon on Friday before the fog lifted sufficiently for fishing to resume but, in any case, we never sighted a single fish until night was falling. Unfortunately, we lost it in the gathering gloom, and so returned to the factory empty-handed for bunkers.

It was now two months today since I had left home, and I felt the time was passing much more quickly now. We caught four more fish today, the total for all catchers being twenty-two. When the mate was dressing my neck today, he said that it was now looking very much better. Later, when we were all returning to the mess for coffee, I caught sight of a Norwegian catcher from another expedition coming across our stern at full speed from the port side. When I read the name, 'Star XVI' aloud, the gunner and the mate immediately reacted. They began shouting out in Norwegian and rushed to the starboard side where the vessel was now running alongside us. A rope was thrown to her and both vessels stopped engines.

It transpired that the gunner on Star XVI had been top gunner with Salvesen the previous season, and our mate's brother was now one of his crew. Having retired to my bunk, I was not aware when the visitors left, but I expect it would have been in the early hours. We had already received a message earlier in the evening, instructing us to return to the factory. It was expected that we would be holding whales next day in view of the recent large number of catches.

When I wakened the next morning, I found (as expected) that we were lying off the factory. We were holding no less than eleven whales. Two penguins were playing about on one of them, and at such close quarters, it was very entertaining watching their antics. I learned today that the catcher, MV Sluga, had been on fire a day or two earlier. MacDonald was the R/O on-board and I realised in retrospect that I may have witnessed the fire. At the time, I had thought it was excess smoke from the funnel.

We were very thankful when the factory relieved us of our holdings as the smell from them was, once again, horrendous. However, as we were about to leave, several catchers came in with more carcases to hold. It wasn't until the early hours of the following morning that we once again got rid of our holdings and were allowed to go out fishing once more. Orders were eventually given out that no more than two whales per boat had to be taken today, and no humpbacks at all. This was to allow the factory to catch up with the work in hand and ensure there would be no danger of carcases going bad. It transpired, however, that the orders became superfluous. A very bad fog developed and only one fish in total was caught.

The gunner and the mate would often come up to listen to the radio in the evening. In the course of one of our early conversations, the mate had asked me if I knew that my name (Anderson) was Swedish. However, had it been spelled 'Andersen', with a second 'e', it would be Norwegian. On being asked if this would be my first Christmas away from home, I answered, "*Yes,*" and he told me that he had spent only one Christmas at home since he was 15 years old. The gunner informed us that his last Christmas at home had been in 1924 when I was only 4 years old.

Messages and instructions could come at any time. One evening, the factory called me with a message stating that we had to circle around her throughout the night. This was to ensure that no icebergs were drifting as she powered up her engines. Thus, if she had to move, it would have to be with our assistance.

A regular task for me again involved the use of the Direction Finder (DF). Going on watch at 6 a.m. one day, I discovered that the DF was not operating correctly. Signals were faint and it was quite impossible to get a sharp, definite bearing. Thinking that the batteries might be at fault, I put them on charge and informed the gunner of the breakdown. However, on my way, I happened to look up at the DF aerial and the cause of the breakdown became clear. The aerial was an old-fashioned type, called a 'birdcage' aerial, for obvious reasons. It was built on the roof of my cabin and consisted of a wooden framework about eight feet high and four feet square. It had eight or nine spaced turns of wire encircling each of the framework's opposite sides. The dampness of the fog, coupled with the freezing spray from the sea had resulted in a coating of ice, making the wires several times their normal diameter, and thus the cause of the trouble.

There was no easy solution for this, so I had to climb up on the framework, one side at a time, then holding on with one hand and with a pair of pliers in the other, I had to laboriously chip the ice off each individual strand of wire. It was, of course, a bitterly cold and very tedious job as it was still a foggy and miserable day. With the constant rolling of the ship, I was kept looking down into the sea, first on one side and then the other, hence the requirement to keep hanging on with one hand during the entire operation. Eventually, however, the job was completed and I gladly returned to the relative warmth of my cabin. My relief was complete when, after midday,

I was able to get a good bearing for the factory. Due to these weather conditions, the factory only received one whale today.

Once again, we were taking on bunkers from the factory in the early hours of the morning, and our personal list of requirements from the slop chest was duly delivered on-board. It turned out that everybody got what they requested, but all my requests were scored out! I was determined to try and get on Sevilla personally the first chance I could get. I felt they must surely have some of the items I wanted. As it was now late into December, the steward had also received our Christmas fare, the main item being a piece of pork, which would be a great change from whale meat. However, somewhat surprisingly, the latter is not too bad.

The foggy weather we had been experiencing continued and the sea was very rough resulting in my being sick for the first time since joining Sirra. That said, I was still able to eat fairly well. Because of the stormy weather, my belongings were scattered all over my cabin and the drawers below my bunk were always sliding out. Fortunately, it improved a bit at night, and by supper time, I was feeling okay again.

Only two days away from Christmas 1939 and it was a lovely day. It was also a successful one for fishing, with a total of twenty-one fish caught. We, however, did not contribute directly as we spent the day collecting the catches from the others and delivering them to the factory. This was due to the factory clearing the previous backlog of whales and wanting prompt delivery of any catches. This practice allowed the other catchers to keep on fishing without returning to the factory, which, of course, suited them. The total catch for this week was eighty-three, of which forty were blues. At night, I heard a radio programme from San Francisco. A Gospel singer, with organ accompaniment, sang a selection of Christmas hymns. It was most enjoyable and of course made my thoughts go homewards once again.

On Christmas Eve 1939, after borrowing the necessary items from the steward, I cleaned and polished my cabin in the forenoon. In the course of conversation, he mentioned that he had not spent Christmas at home for twenty-four years! At 7:30 p.m., we had our Christmas dinner, which was very good indeed, consisting of pork chops with potatoes, cabbage and cranberries, followed by rice, canned fruit and whipped cream. I had to temporarily leave the mess room after the main course as I had to go on watch at 8 p.m. It was routine to listen out for any possible requests or instructions from the factory. I soon returned for a short time to eagerly finish my repast.

During the course of the evening, I had to take several bearings of the factory as it became foggy again. I also received instructions that we had to patrol around the factory again during the night, keeping a look-out for icebergs. This was coupled with seasonal greetings and best wishes from Sevilla's captain. I re-joined the others in the mess at 10 p.m. when we had tea, dough rings and biscuits. Apples, oranges and nuts were also made available.

It was a very pleasant end to the evening and I returned to my cabin between 11 p.m. and midnight. The gunner, mate and chief engineer said they would be coming up to listen to the radio. I wasn't sorry when they did not appear as I had to get up as usual at 5:45 a.m. I thought they may have 'refreshed' themselves too much! Although some catchers had actually encountered whales today, the total catch was only one blue and two others.

Even though it was Christmas Day, fishing went on as usual. We had a good breakfast of bacon and eggs, which had been kept over from yesterday – Sunday being the usual day for that dish. However, when I say 'eggs', I have to explain they are the produce of 'birds' peculiar to this part of the world, i.e., penguins! The steward had a large box of them which had been gathered at South Georgia and it lay on the boat-deck outside my cabin. Also, he kept his supply of whale meat hanging there, cutting off a piece as he needed it.

To return to the eggs, these were always made into omelettes with pieces of bacon or meat added, plus some milk to tone them down a bit as they were fairly strong in flavour. I took one from the box to blow out the contents and had difficulty in making holes in the thick shell, and much more so when it came to the blowing part.

After breakfast, I was on the bridge when, to my surprise, the gunner asked,

"Sparks, would you like to take a spell at the wheel?"

I was particularly quick with my reply of *'Yes'*, *as* the adrenalin was pumping even before he had finished his question. I had wrongly anticipated that I was going to be offered a chance to fire the harpoon gun. I had earlier learned that the position of gunner was highly prized and protected from infiltration by outsiders. Generally, it was confined to families, being handed from father to son. Also, in Salvesen's case at least, they were all of Norwegian nationality. I had earlier been teased a bit about firing the gun, and later there was a moment when I thought the Christmas spirit, or perhaps the other kind, was going to facilitate some temporary entry to that inner circle. However, it was not to be. I later consoled myself with the thought … *'What if I had missed?'*

Anyway, our catch for the day was two, the factory total being fourteen with two blue. At night, when delivering our second fish, we were instructed to tow in the catcher MV Sarna, which had engine trouble. We sighted her about 10 p.m. when she sent a message saying that temporary repairs had been carried out and she was going to collect a flagged whale that had drifted away. When we reached her, she was standing by her catch which we took in tow, and at the same time, passed two ropes from our stern to her bow allowing us to return to the factory, with Sarna partly under her own power.

The sea was very calm on Boxing Day and it was afternoon before we sighted and caught our first fish. Leaving her flagged, we set off in chase of another. A hit was made, but unfortunately, the arms or hooks of the harpoon had not opened out, so the harpoon came out. Thankfully, we eventually made up on and secured it with another harpoon, some three hours after first taking up the chase.

On returning to pick up our first whale, we found that it was surrounded by small killer whales. The mate called them 'speckle hawks', possibly because of the whitish-looking spots on their bodies. They were about ten to fifteen feet in length. Being one of the few types with teeth, they were engaged in eating the tongue of our catch. They followed us for quite a time after we took the fish in tow. As the head of our catch reached our stern, we could see them quite clearly milling about and going after the tongue. From time to time, they were jumping clean out of the water. The mate tried to scare them off with the aid of a boat hook but without success.

Although quite stormy, we were amongst pack ice where the sea was calmer. There were a great many seals lying on the ice. The following day was the finest day we have yet experienced with the sea very much calmer under a blue sky and shining sun. However, it still felt very cold. In the morning, we chased a large whale for nearly three hours, but it proved to have a faster turn of speed than us, so we had to give up the chase. However, we did get a blue at night. On the following day, we passed within sight of South Orkney Island which lies sixty degrees south of the equator. We could clearly see many large mountain peaks but sadly, no fish. I heard on the radio today that Admiral Byrd had left New Zealand and was bound for the Antarctic.

Hogmanay, 31st December 1939. At 8:45 p.m., I was sitting in my cabin listening to London and the sounds of the bringing-in of the New Year at home. The sky was clear, the sea calm, and we were within sight of the factory. We were on our way back from the pack ice with one blue which we had chased for about two and a half hours. I wondered if my folks at home would be sitting up and listening to the Midnight Service which I was happy to know was coming from Scotland. How I wished I was there.

As the service ended, we were preparing to hand over our fish to the factory, so I decided to have a look around. Given our position at that time, we would not see in the New Year for another two hours and forty minutes. After handing over our whale, we drew alongside for bunkers and our new year stores. This should have been undertaken the previous night, had we not been as far from the factory as we thought. Snow was now falling, albeit not heavily.

When the New Year arrived for us, we were still moored alongside Sevilla. The work of cutting up the whales was continuing unchecked. As there was no indication whatsoever that a new year had arrived, I got into my bunk. The steward, however, had the New Year spirit later when he arrived with a cup of tea and two doughnuts whilst I was keeping my morning watch at 6 a.m. We had bacon and eggs for breakfast this morning and, at lunch, we had roast leg of pork with cranberries which I enjoyed immensely. I had a message from the factory before midday asking us to come in immediately. This was followed at 1 p.m. with an order to all boats to stop fishing. Catches had been so good that they were unable to handle anymore.

My slop chest requirements had come on-board this morning with the stores. However, once again, two items were scored out, namely, sea boots and a camera, which disappointed me. The Sirra lies so low in the water that only on the calmest days can one walk along the deck without the risk of at least getting soaked, thus sea boots would be most useful. As for not having a camera, this was the most disappointing of all. Salt was rubbed into the proverbial wound by the receipt of spools of film for the camera they could not supply. I did not know what I was supposed to do with them, but I was tempted to tell the supplier what *he* could do with them! I resolved to try and get on-board the factory next time we bunkered, providing it was not during the early hours of the morning. Weather-wise, this was a lovely day and at night we had a red sunset.

Tuesday 2nd January 1940 - My twentieth birthday. If I had been asked less than three months ago, '*Where do you think you will be on your first birthday away from home?*', this place would have been the furthest from my thoughts. However, as my father had said to me on my departure, how fortunate I was to get this opportunity, participating in an expedition to such a romantic area, associated with memories of Scott, Shackleton, Amundsen and Byrd. My father also told me that one thing I must do was to keep a diary, and he had given me three eight-by-five-inch notebooks and three pencils for the purpose.

The notebooks were soon filled, but it was not possible to replace them, and notepaper could not be easily had. In the end, I was reduced to opening out old envelopes and boxes to write on the inside. This had some relevance to the delays in my endeavouring to finally transcribe these scribbled notes into a legible form more than fifty-seven years later. In truth, I feel very sad now, and quite ashamed, that my father was never to see and read the result of what he instigated.

At breakfast this morning, firstly the mate, followed by the others, stood up and shook my hand, being aware it was my birthday. We were holding whales today and I took the opportunity to wash some clothes down in the engine room, which was the only place to get hot water. It was also the place for gossip, and I was told that one of the firemen was very drunk as a result of drinking a mixture of Hammerslag, Benzene and Brilliantine. A very potent mixture!

When I got up next morning, we were still holding. I discovered that another of Salvesen's ships, the SS Strombus, had arrived during the night and was lying alongside the factory. She was taking some of our whale oil back to South Georgia. After we handed over some whales to the factory, I was sitting listening to the radio about 10 a.m. when suddenly the door opened and in came the mate with letters in his hand.

There were five letters in all, and I seized them eagerly. Initially, I was somewhat disappointed to discover none were from home, however, there was one from my Uncle William in Lanarkshire. The others were from friends and made very enjoyable reading before going down for lunch at 11:30 a.m. When I arrived at the mess room, only the chief engineer was there and he had also received five letters from Norway which, somewhat surprisingly, had not been censored.

The steward gave us more good news by telling us that after we had delivered the last of the whales, we were to get some parcels which the Strombus had also brought. I was quite excited by this and wondered if there would be one for me, perhaps with a letter included. My nerves got the better of me and, after waiting on deck for a time, I decided that if I was going to be disappointed, then, like Greta Garbo, '*I wanted to be alone*', so retired to my cabin.

At midday, I was preparing my codes and writing materials for the usual 12:30 p.m. reports, when suddenly there was a loud cry of, "*Sparks!*" I rushed out, and standing there was the steward with three parcels, all for me! Despite my excitement and desperately wishing to open them straight away, I decided to wait until after my watch was completed. Then I could lie on my bunk and open them at leisure, without interruption. During my watch, we had delivered the last of the whales and set off once again to re-commence fishing. It was becoming foggy again and light snow was falling as we headed for the ice.

As soon as my watch was over, I hurriedly opened up the parcels and was delighted to find there were letters included with the contents. Everything was simply perfect and I could not have wished for more. I was especially delighted that my mother's home-baking constituted the bulk of the contents. This was equally appreciated by my mess-room mates, including the steward, who were high in their praise of the shortbread and cakes of various kinds. I did not, however, produce the entire contents on the first day. I decided it would be better to put a little out each day at afternoon coffee time for as long as they lasted. This, of course, met with the approval and delight of my companions.

I received orders during the evening that we had to do iceberg patrol around the factory again tonight, so I took a bearing of it before having an early night. I lay in my bunk looking at the lovely Christmas card which my mother had sent, and which looked so well against the white paintwork on the wall. I thought, *'what a wonderful day this has been'*, and of course, I thought of my loved ones at home, who now felt a little closer to me.

I was wakened twice during the night, firstly, to take another bearing of the factory at 1:30 a.m., and again at 4.40 a.m. when the mate called to tell me that the aerial had snapped and was lying on deck. However, he said he would fix it himself if I could assure him that he would not be in danger of getting a shock. This I was very pleased to do. The weather was very bad at this time with a rough sea as well as thick fog. It had forced the Strombus to cast off from the factory, and both ships then moved into calmer waters off the pack ice. Because of weather conditions, no whales were caught today. In the evening, we were instructed to stand-by Strombus and the catcher MV Shika, to attend the factory.

On Friday, the Strombus was able to go alongside the factory again, and the transfer of cargoes resumed. Throughout the day, we kept up our patrol and kept the larger ice floes away from the two ships, until they parted company again during the evening. Around 10 p.m., I visited the chief engineer in his cabin to tell him that there was a good play on the radio. As he switched on his own set, I heard a message from the Strombus breaking through to the factory. They were requesting we transfer one of their messboys back from the factory where he had been stranded when the two ships had parted earlier. I returned up on deck to warn the gunner. As I arrived, the factory called us in, so we collected the boy at the same time, whilst arranging to come right back for bunkers.

On our return to the factory, I saw a messboy standing at an open door in the ship's side below the main deck, so I shouted up to him,

"Have they any cameras in the slop chest?" to which he answered,

"Yes ... plenty!"

As the slop chest was not open at that time of night, I gave the boy a note to hand in the next day - this being the third time I had ordered a camera.

I also asked the boy to try and get me a whale's tooth and an eardrum from below decks. Whilst we were still alongside, the catcher MV Sahra arrived and put one of their firemen on-board the factory. Apparently, he was unable to cope with life on a catcher and particularly its gyrations in rough weather. The Strombus left later to call on other expeditions.

I have little to relate apart from the fact that very few whales are being caught. After one month's fishing, we have processed only about 28,000 barrels of oil, and the daylight hours are getting shorter in number. Our quota for three months of fishing is 99,000 barrels. We returned to bunkers again on Tuesday, when I was able to call at the slop chest personally, but only to receive the old story ... *'none left!'*

The following day, my DF was out of order, and by working on it most of the day, I missed the finest afternoon we have had. It was like a summer's day and, in the evening, there was a lovely sunset with a rose-pink sky. Catches were good today with a total of twenty-one blue and three fin. We, however, were only collecting and bringing in flagged whales.

The Strombus called back today and we were told to put two of our holding whales alongside the factory to act as fenders. After handing over the last of our holding whales, we were fishing again by 10 a.m. It was lovely weather at first but it did not last long. On the following morning, we were on our own, about seventy to eighty miles away and, although foggy, we sighted a good many fish. On reporting this, the other boats, having seen nothing themselves, headed for our locality. Unfortunately, the fog worsened, and although we managed to get one fish, we lost sight of the others. Sorsa, rated the top catcher, also got one, but the other boats were too late in arriving.

The fog remained throughout Saturday, but on Sunday, although foggy within the pack ice, it was clearer in the open sea, and whales had been sighted. We had begun chasing when I received orders that we were required to bring in flagged fish. Afterwards, we had to stand-by, holding. The gunner, of course, was never happy in this situation. So, in an attempt to keep his blood pressure under control, he began making a fishing-net for somewhat smaller fish.

It was Tuesday before we handed over the last of the whales. As these were getting somewhat scarce again, we were directed to go off on our own to search and attempt to locate some. The next morning, when we were about 100 miles away from the factory, I reported that we had seen a great many whales. At 9 a.m., I received a message telling us to stop where we were and not to go any further away. At this time, we were fairly close to pack ice and the second engineer came up with the suggestion,

"What about trying to get a bit of fresh meat, or rather, liver?"

According to him, seal meat was a great delicacy. This met with the general approval of his fellow countrymen, so it was into the ice in search. There were a good number of seals to be seen, but on this occasion, they must have been mind-readers because, as we approached the ice floes on which they rested, they each in turn plunged into the sea to escape. Eventually, we came upon one which appeared to be sleeping and even when we nosed-up against its floe, it never budged. However, up to this point, no one had apparently thought of how the seal was to be dispatched.

The mate offered to jump onto the floe and use a boat hook, but this was considered to be too dangerous. It was not a very large floe, and therefore, could be quite unstable. It was decided to use the whale gun but loaded solely with the charge plus the wadding used for the ejection of the harpoon. Upon this being fired, it had no apparent effect beyond giving the seal the fright of its life. It promptly vacated the floe for the safety of the sea, with a new-found agility that had to be seen to be believed.

After a few minutes, however, the seal re-appeared and clambered onto another ice floe some distance away, towards which we slowly made our way. Meantime, there was some further discussion as to what type of ammunition should now be attempted. This set two engineers running off to the engine room to find something suitable. Their makeshift ammo was duly loaded into the gun. We did not approach so closely this time as the seal was now on the alert and, in any case, it was considered that this charge would be sufficient.

The gunner appeared to score a direct hit, but to everyone's amazement, the seal once again charged off the ice floe and into the sea. However, it was unable to stay under and a tell-tale trail of red confirmed the hit. Most unfortunately, we had to give up the pursuit with no chance to recover the poor animal. I did regret, however, that we did not have a chance to see it delivered from its agony, although it would not have lasted long. Afterwards, there was a sense of shame hanging over the ship. The incident was never referred to, nor was there any attempt to repeat it!

It was now nearly midday and the gunner told me to contact the factory and ask permission to commence fishing. The answer was in the negative, and we were asked to return. It was 7:30 p.m. when we arrived within sight of the other catchers and received orders to start fishing. By this time, however, it was too late as darkness was falling, which was unfortunate as there were plenty of whales around.

Next morning, we began fishing early and had already caught three by 9:30 a.m. when I got a message telling us to stop fishing and return to the factory. When I gave the message to the gunner, he was furious. As there were many fish around, he told me to reply that we were fast to a fish. On doing so, I got the reply to come in as soon as it was caught. Fortunately for us, we were, in fact, fast to one shortly afterwards, and returned to the factory after collecting our other three fish.

By 12:30 p.m., twenty-four fish had been caught with another fast. Later in the afternoon, when the total had reached thirty-four, all boats were ordered to stop fishing. I learned that the Sahra had caught nine, and Sorsa, six. At 10 p.m., we were instructed to tow the factory towards the area where the catchers had been mainly operating. It was a lovely night, and at sunset, the sky was red with streaks of pink, green, blue and yellow. It was quite magnificent … and me without a camera!

I had an unexpected but very welcome surprise when we were temporarily alongside the factory for the night. My obliging friend, the messboy, hailed me from the top deck of the factory. Quickly shinning down a rope ladder, he presented me with a paper bag. To my sheer delight, on opening same, I discovered that it contained not one, but two whale's teeth, one large and one small, as well as one eardrum. It made my day.

I had almost given up hope that I would be fortunate enough to get such marvellous and rare souvenirs. The eardrum is a bony structure about the size and shape of a good-sized clenched fist. In fact, it is not unlike a conch shell and, when seen, often mistaken for such. When viewed side-on, it indeed looked remarkably like a human face in profile. This effect is enhanced by penning in an eye to the socket-like depression in the bone.

Today, Friday 19th January, was spent holding for the factory, and fishing was again stopped after another twenty fish had been caught. Next day, we kept holding until the afternoon, when we were able to resume fishing once again. The sea was now a bit rough with a heavy swell. We had sighted and were chasing a blue, when I received an order for us to return to a holding position once again.

At about 10:15 p.m., I was in my bunk when the gunner appeared and asked me if I knew the call sign of the radio station on South Georgia. On replying that I was not too sure but could easily get it from the factory, he asked me to do just that. He then added that we were going there. I could see that he was not in a happy frame of mind, but he did not volunteer any further information. After getting the necessary call signs, I returned to my bunk.

Next morning, I was very abruptly wakened at 5:30 a.m. by a blow on the side of my face, followed by something crashing onto the floor. The object which had struck me turned out to be my alarm clock, and on the floor was my water bottle. On getting out of my bunk and looking out of the porthole, I could see that we were heading at full speed into a rough sea. It was also snowing as well as being foggy. When on watch at 6:30 a.m., I learned the reason for our journey by over-hearing the factory in conversation with one of the other catchers. We were apparently taking one of their crewmen to the hospital on South Georgia, him being a suspected appendicitis case.

At breakfast, the gunner gave me a report to send back to the factory stating that we were experiencing bad weather with heavy snow and that the sick man, Pedersen, was '*okay*'. When I later took reports along to the gunner's cabin, I found that Pedersen was lying on the settee and, although looking a little pale, he seemed otherwise to be alright. Meanwhile, the gunner was examining a sextant which, from its green and mouldy appearance, had not seen the light of day for some considerable time. I got the feeling that he was beginning to worry about our position, as I had been unable to contact either LTH (Leith Harbour) or ZBH (Grytviken) stations. The sextant was not of much use at the time anyway, the sun being invisible because of the fog.

Although I was still able to communicate with the factory last night, this morning I could only hear her very faintly, and was unable to make actual contact. At 7.30 a.m., the coast of South Georgia was sighted and I stayed on the bridge most of the morning as it was such a glorious day. The sun was shining from a blue sky, and it was feeling so much warmer. The island presented a fine appearance together with her shore-based fleet. We sailed into Leith Harbour after our four-hundred-and-forty-mile journey and, to our surprise, found our arrival was unexpected. It was around 1.30 p.m. that Pedersen, our patient, was able to travel the short distance to the hospital on foot.

I took the chance to call at the secretary's office to see if I could get a camera. Alas, the office was closed. I was unable to wait as the Sirra was going around to Stromness to re-fuel. When we were taking on fuel, I decided to go ashore to have a good look around. Happily, Stromness was more attractive than Leith Harbour. In the past, it used to operate as a shore-based whaling station but was now unused except for oil storage.

I saw sea lions again and also one of the extremely large king penguins. This only brought back the agonies of still being without a camera. It is interesting to know that it was from here that Salvesen ships had, over the years, collected penguins, including the king variety, to replenish as required the resident species at Edinburgh Zoo.

When I returned from my walk, the mate was doing a bit of fishing. He was standing at the rail with a length of cord to which was attached a treble hook but without bait. Once the hook was let down a few feet into the very clear water, he pulled it up and down in jerking movements and the fish, apparently attracted by the shining hooks, became impaled on them. The mate had a bucketful in no time at all and the steward immediately whipped them off to the galley in preparation for our tea.

The steward told me later that the skins were so thick that he had to skin them prior to their preparation for cooking. However, it was a great treat to get such fresh food, which we enjoyed immensely. One of the fish caught but not used was a most peculiar specimen, being nearly all head with little or no body, and was completely transparent.

After bunkering, we returned to Leith Harbour, only to be told that we had to report to the Magistrate at Grytviken before we could leave the island. This was the site of the Argentinian whaling station, positioned further round the coast. It was nicely situated, with more attractive buildings than at Leith Harbour. Close to the harbour stands a cross erected in the memory of Sir Ernest Shackleton, the famous explorer.

When shipwrecked on the Antarctic ice, he made his way, with his crew and a lifeboat, to a point where they could row to South Georgia. Having landed on its uninhabited side, and despite their poor condition, he made an epic journey over the high snow-covered mountains, eventually reaching Grytviken station. It was the first occasion that this had ever been accomplished! Shackleton, whilst embarking on a later expedition, died in his bunk from natural causes at Grytviken, shortly after arriving back from Great Britain.

Whilst we were awaiting the gunner's return from the Magistrate's office, a man came on-board, and, to my great surprise, he turned out to be the one and only policeman on the island. He hailed from Edinburgh and had only recently arrived. When asked what he did in such an isolated place, his reply was that, so far, it was to lock up the occasional drunken Argentinian whaler. After a night in the cell, he would simply release them again in the morning. On the gunner's return, complete with clearance permission, we set off on our 500-mile return journey to re-join the expedition. By 7:30 p.m., we found ourselves back in the fog once more.

Next day, 23rd January, I was able to hear the factory transmitting very faintly at 6.30 a.m. and, on Wednesday morning, we arrived in the vicinity of the other catchers. I informed the factory that we expected to reach her about midday. In reply, I was given the instructions that we were to collect whales from other boats on our way in. The gunner was furious when I told him, as the catchers were spread over a large area. So, after collecting three fish, and still trying to make up on the Sarna, he told me to call the factory. I was to say (with some exaggeration) that Sarna was still forty miles away. As a result, the reply was to come in with the three whales we had already collected. It was 10:30 p.m. when we eventually reached the factory.

When I wakened next morning, we were leaving the factory with instructions to guide another of the Company's supply ships, SS Coronda, through the heavy pack ice and back to the factory. Later, when talking to the chief engineer in my cabin, I heard shouting. On looking out of the porthole, I saw the gunner throwing lumps of coal at some unknown, distant target. Going on deck, we saw that this was, in fact, a poor, innocent seal that just happened to be on a floe which we had come against. The chief instinctively ran to the steward's storage bin, filled his pockets with potatoes and, on returning, joined the gunner in some target practice. The seal, who did not move an inch, simply roared defiance at its assailants as the ship moved on. It was soon surrounded by coal and potatoes as if part of some surreal ritual.

I finished writing letters home today and was thankful the mate was able to supply me with envelopes for same. Hopefully, the Coronda, or some other ship, will take them back to the UK. As we are now halfway through the fishing season, we are to get a new gunner on-board tonight for the second half. On the following day, we caught three blue, but later on, were put onto holding duties once again. These past few days, the early mornings have been perfect weather-wise, but it has always deteriorated later in the day, and we are also experiencing more snow. Over the weekend and into Monday were quiet fishing days. On Monday, I had my hair cut by 'Shetland', a deckhand who originated from one of Shetland's small isles which, if I recall correctly, may have been called Burra.

We learned the next day of a very sad incident on-board the catcher, Sahra. The mate had been engaged in loading the gun in preparation for a second firing when there was an explosion. The harpoon ejection plug was blown out, resulting in serious injuries to his hands.

We did not return to the factory that night and, at 7:30 a.m., we caught a fin, but nothing else was seen that day. It was 8:30 p.m. before we returned to hand over our catch. On this being accomplished, we were instructed to make an expedition up to one hundred miles southwest by west from the factory, and report anything of interest.

Wednesday turned out to be a lovely day with the sun shining in the morning, but we sighted no whales. In the afternoon, when we were approaching our one-hundred-mile limit, I received a signal from the factory saying to wait for a message. This turned out to be an order to return immediately for the purpose of taking the injured mate to the hospital at Leith Harbour. However, when it was known that we were so far away, the message was cancelled and the Shika was delegated to take over the task. We began fishing once more but it was now snowing, visibility was bad and we had still had no sightings.

It was still snowing the next day, accompanied by continuing poor visibility. At midday, we were fast to a blue, but unfortunately, we suffered a break and lost it. Early in the afternoon, I felt a thud and knew that we had collided with something, but it didn't seem to be ice. This was confirmed on going down for coffee. Apparently, Shetland had been left alone on the bridge and, on observing what he described as *'two or three queer-looking creatures'* on the surface, he altered course and headed the ship straight towards them.

The 'creatures' turned out to be very ordinary sperm whales. However, they often lie on the surface for long periods and, in some confusion, he had taken the ship right over one of them. This resulted in it being hit by the propeller. Shetland rightly received a very strong dressing-down for his most foolish action and was made well aware of the dangers to both ship and crew!

The third day of February was a nice day, and we sighted many whales. At 9 a.m., I heard the factory contacting Shika and being told that the South Georgia doctor had said that he might be able to save both the mate's hands. However, he would have to wait two or three days before he could be certain about the left one in particular. Shika returned on Sunday after delivering the injured but recovering mate. Regretfully, there was no additional mail. When I got into my bunk that night, I found that somehow, a potato had mysteriously found its way under my bottom blanket. This was not to be the last time that strange things were to occur!

After a quiet day on Monday, we sighted and began chasing several fish the following afternoon. I had just received orders to collect flagged whales when I heard our gun go off. We had it secured quickly and proceeded to collect the others for the factory. Alas, when we finally reached them, we were immediately put on holding duty. A total of thirty-two fish had been caught, comprising twenty-eight fin and four blue.

We continued holding through Wednesday but were able to leave next morning at 9 a.m. and resume fishing once more. We caught nothing, however, being hampered by heavy rain and thick mist. In the evening, we were served some of our stock of whale meat, and I must say that it was very nice. I would not have known the difference between whale meat and the bovine variety. After supper, entertainment amounted to playing cards until late.

In the morning, the gunner called and asked me to contact the factory to see if we would be allowed to take more sperm whales. The answer was a definitive, *'No!'* I later learned that there were no less than five in number already caught. As I had to take down a long, coded message, I lost the chance to see my first sperm whale. The weather was slightly improved on Saturday, but yet, once again, we spent most of the day collecting.

It was now only four more weeks until the end of the fishing season. The mist persisted and we were sent out to collect two fish from Sahra, but when we reached her, we were told that they had lost them in the mist. We searched around, eventually finding one, which we delivered to the factory. It was still quite misty the next day and I spent a great deal of time at the DF because of that. Sorsa reported that she had come across Sahra's missing fish, and we were instructed to collect and deliver it to the factory.

When we reached Sorsa, however, they said they were delivering the whale themselves, so we began fishing again.

Shortly afterwards, we had sighted two blue and were chasing them when I received a message from the factory saying they wanted to move and required our services. When I returned to my bunk at night, I discovered yet another mysterious happening. This time, there was no potato in my bunk, but a not-inconsiderable chunk of iron! I still had no clue who or what was responsible.

On Tuesday, I learned that the Coronda was coming down again from Leith Harbour. It looks as if my letters home would not arrive there any sooner than I would. It was my understanding that she was going straight back to the UK after her last visit here, but obviously not. Next day, the factory flag was flying at half-mast as a mark of respect to one of their Watchmen who had died on-board.

By Friday, the weather had begun to deteriorate, with a southerly wind making it much colder. We were chasing whales most of the day but found them a bit too fast for our old engine. Sirra, being one of the few older catchers in service, did not have the turn of speed of the newer versions. Lists were distributed from the factory asking for names of anyone willing to over-winter at Leith Harbour at the end of the season. I had been giving it some consideration but decided not to volunteer. With this having been my first trip at sea, family bonds were still too strong for an extended trip.

The weather worsened considerably and we found ourselves within a circle of ice for most of the day. The factory called me saying that we were to come out of the ice and tow her back in. When we got out of the protective area of ice, we experienced the worst seas yet. Very strong winds, accompanied by blinding snow, were tossing the boat about like a cork. Later, the wind increased to gale force and the seas became even bigger, making progress hopeless. The factory again impatiently called us to come and take them to safety off the ice, but the gunner's reply was that we were having to lie-to. If the factory could come to us, we could lead them to safety. I got the abrupt reply, *"Get back to the ice, but you remain on watch!"*

However, the fact was, we were now facing the oncoming waves and the gale head-on, so we could not make any progress whatsoever. It was, for me, a dreadful experience that I would never wish to repeat. The height of the waves was unbelievable, and I had to try and jam myself into the chair at my desk as best I could. It was a nightmare. One minute I would be looking through my forward-facing porthole at the heavens above, before shuddering momentarily, and plunging down with a crash into the seemingly bottomless trough of the wave. This meant there was an even more frightening sight then facing me through the porthole.

Would the time arrive when we did not rise again from this dreadful abyss? Before long, however, we would be borne up again with the sea breaking over the bow, making the boat awash with spray coming right over my cabin at the stern. Whilst that gave momentary relief, the cycle continued relentlessly. During this time, it was almost impossible to hold a pencil in my hand to take down messages. One hand was trying to keep myself (and the chair) at my desk, whilst fending off loose flying objects including code books and papers, etc.

The spare chair was completely smashed to pieces from being thrown from wall to wall behind me. Powerless to do anything about it until the following day, I simply had to throw the pieces overboard. I was, of course, sick throughout the whole process. Fortunately, I had made some provision for that very eventuality by having a large empty biscuit tin, which had been used to protect the eatables in one of my Christmas parcels. However, once used, it could not be allowed to fly about, so I had kept it precariously grasped between my thighs.

Mercifully, at 11 p.m., the factory told me that I could go off-watch. So, with great difficulty, I managed to drag myself into my bunk, realising that I couldn't have carried on much longer. What a blessed relief it was to be lying down!

By the next day, we had made practically no headway, and we were still many miles away from the safety of the ice. I was not yet feeling too good but did manage to take some breakfast. Unfortunately, on returning to my cabin, it and I soon parted company. After the 8:30 a.m. reports, I returned to my bunk until lunch at 11:30 a.m. After the 12:30 p.m. reports, I repeated the action. However, after a mug of tea at 3:30 p.m., I was back to square one. I finally got up at 6:45 p.m. when we had, by this time, reached some ice and the seas were much calmer. Unfortunately, I happened to notice that one of the wires on the DF aerial had snapped and so I had, once again, to clamber up on top of the cabin roof to repair it.

As before, it proved to be a hazardous task as it was still snowing with a very strong wind blowing. After reports at 7:30 p.m., I washed and headed down for supper, which I was thankfully able to take and retain. At this time, we were engaged in chasing a single blue. However, due to the snow and the failing light, we had to give up the chase. It was just as well, as the harpoon gun and all the fore-end of the ship were, by this time, fully encased in ice.

The weather on the following day was generally much better, but still very cold with a strong wind and occasional heavy snow. On Wednesday, the factory was steaming west at full speed when whales were sighted, so she stopped. A total of twenty-two fish were caught by the others, but we were unsuccessful. Our decks and rails were still thickly encrusted with ice.

Thursday was a fine, mild day and the sea was like a pond. At night, we were alongside getting bunkers and I decided to go to the secretary's office, but stopped when I reached the top of the ladder. I found, to my dismay, that there were piles of whale meat lying right along and against the ship's side. It was impossible to step over and too deep to walk through. So, somewhat rashly, I decided to jump across it from the ship's rail. I got over the meat alright, but when my feet hit the blood-soaked deck, they shot up in the air, and I landed flat on my back. Soaked to the skin from head to heels, I had no alternative but to precariously wade back through the meat. Woefully, I made my way back down the rope ladder, and then to my cabin for a wash and change of clothes. Alas, the story did not end there!

Having changed, I was walking along to the galley for a bucket of water in which to soak my soiled clothes. At this time, we were drawing away from the side of the factory, having completed our bunkering. Suddenly, and without warning, there was an almighty 'crash' and 'splash'. A member of the factory crew, no doubt thinking that we were cleared from their side, had thrown overboard a bucketful of 'whale filth' including blood and bones. It landed right on top of me! Some of the contents had even gone into the bucket I was carrying and unfortunately, one piece of bone hit the top of my right foot. As I was only wearing slippers at the time, it was quite painful and soon swelled up. If it had hit me on my head, I'm sure it would have knocked me out.

In the morning, I washed the soiled clothes, but more bad luck was to befall me. For some unknown reason, I was sitting on top of my desk and, leaning back, I smashed one of the valves on the radio. However, very fortunately, I happened to have a replacement.

This was a dull and dirty day with a mixture of snow showers and rain. We chased after three fish but made no contact. It was very misty all through Saturday and no whales were caught. Whilst chatting with the second engineer, he informed me that he had received word that he was required to over-winter at Leith Harbour. I also learned today that by this stage in the expedition, the factory had now processed 90,015 barrels of oil.

Because of fog, no fishing was possible through both Sunday and Monday. On the latter day, between 11 p.m. and midnight, I was listening to the radio. I was about to switch it off when I heard the loud cry of, *"Sparks!"*.

In walked Jorgen, the mate, accompanied by the chief engineer. Immediately, I could smell alcohol, and told them so. They proceeded to spin me a story that they had been visiting the gunner who wanted to see me as he had lost the factory in the fog. I told them that I would see the gunner in the morning, and that they should go away and let me sleep. Things became a bit awkward as the chief switched on the transmitter and began to operate the Morse key. I managed to get the mate to one side and implored him, with hushed voice and signals, to get the chief out of the cabin. Eventually he did, and thankfully, both departed.

Then, around 1 a.m., I was abruptly wakened by my cabin door bursting open. A large figure appeared and filled the doorway before staggering in. It was the mate, Jorgen. He could hardly speak a word, and I could not make any sense out of him whatsoever. After some time, I managed to see him safely out. However, I did push him out into heavy snow which was being blown almost horizontally across the stern in the strong wind. I was just relieved to eventually get my door shut. This time, however, I bolted the door before getting back into my bunk, the disturbance quelled. Or so I thought.

When I arose in the morning and stepped onto the floor, I could not believe my eyes. There was a terrible mess all over the floor which, at first, I could not fathom or understand. It was an unknown squelchy mass of equally unknown origin. On closer examination, it was soon revealed that these were, or had been at some stage, potatoes. But, I wondered, what on earth had caused them to be in such a state? I stared at the scene for a while before the answer to this conundrum eventually dawned on me.

The cabin door had a brass circular vent with open segments to the outside, and a moveable, inner plate with similar open segments. These could be manually rotated to close or open the vent to the outside air. I would usually have these in the open position. It would appear that my erstwhile visitors had later returned. Unable to get in through the (now bolted) cabin door, they must have retreated to the deck below and availed themselves of potato 'ammunition' from the nearby steward's supply box. Oblivious in my slumber, they must have opened fire, using the door vent as their target. Despite the firing squad's poor physical condition earlier, their aim remained surprisingly good, no doubt aided by the earlier seal practice!

For the next three days, no fishing was possible due to constant thick fog, and we had to stand-by the factory. On Saturday, the weather had improved somewhat. During the night, I had, for reasons unknown, been dreaming about two friends from home, Jack McNee and Jim Cairncross. I could not remember the details, but it seemed to be a chance meeting in a Perth street. I was obviously thinking of home and friends left behind.

On Sunday, we were sent on a short expedition during which we passed fairly close to the SS Nilsen Alonzo and part of a Norwegian expedition. The sea was calm with a long swell and our trip was without success as far as finding whales was concerned. The factory reported the total catch for the day being six fish in all. On Monday, the sea was choppy at first but became rougher by night. I spent some of my free time reading a Penguin book on Scott's last expedition to the Antarctic. Then, from messages I intercepted later on, it seemed that a transport ship was on its way to us.

In the coming days, the weather turned very rough so we were shipping water badly. In such circumstances, and in order to traverse the main deck to the mess, one had to wait until the ship heeled over to the leeward side. Thereafter, it required rushing like mad along the deck and into the mess before she rolled back to windward and shipped more water. Unfortunately, on this particular occasion, I misjudged the ship's roll and was only halfway along when a very heavy sea was shipped. I managed to grab the inboard safety rail in time, failing which I would surely have been washed overboard, both unseen and unheard. As it was, my feet were swept from underneath me and I was momentarily held in a horizontal position at rail height with my feet practically over the ship's side. My only contact with the ship at that time was my grip on the inboard rail. I shall never forget that experience, nor my feelings at that moment!

When the ship rolled back to leeward and my feet were beneath me once again, I very hurriedly managed to scramble up onto the boat deck and along to my cabin. After drying myself and changing clothing, I headed once again for the mess, this time, however, going over the hazards on the boat deck and safely down to join my companions, who, of course, were completely unaware of my adventure. I was certainly more than pleased to be back with them again. I learned later that all the catchers were hove to this day because of the worsening weather conditions.

On returning to my cabin after breakfast the next day, I heard that the Sorsa was calling me. On acknowledging, I learned that she wanted to give me the contents of a telegram addressed to our mate. Apparently, the Sorsa had in turn received it from the Norwegian vessel, SS Suderoy. I was sorry thereafter to be the bearer of bad news for the mate. The message announced the death of his mother back in Norway. He told me that he had not seen her for over eighteen months, as he had previously over-wintered.

The mate's father had also died shortly before he had set off on the 1938/39 season. I did feel very sorry for him.

Later, I overheard the factory telling the supply vessel not to visit her, as they had sufficient fuel left to finish the season. I was very disappointed. This meant that we were unlikely to receive further mail unless some was waiting at Leith Harbour. We took on fuel at night, at which time I took the opportunity of handing over the required end-of-season inventory of all the radio equipment on-board Sirra.

Although the sea condition was very much improved the following day, there was a fairly large swell as we headed homewards through some small, loose ice. The Norwegian factory ships must have reached their quotas as they had ceased fishing. I doubted whether we would manage that now and, despite chasing fish all day, we caught nothing. The sun was shining from a clear blue sky, so perhaps that had something to do with it. Well, that was the excuse I used to use when I would return home empty-handed from fishing the river or loch back home.

There was no sunshine on Saturday. It was the last day of the season, and the sea was back to normal. We were fast to a fish before 8 a.m., but for some unexplained reason, there was no one operating the brake on the line. This meant that we were in great danger of losing the whale, plus all our line along with the harpoon! Fortunately, however, the brake was operated in time and the fish was eventually secured.

It seemed as if our final day was going to be one of misfortune. After being fast to another fish, the harpoon became dislodged, and this was followed by a breaking line on a third target. However, we ended the season with three fish which brought the day's total to twenty-two, all being fin. At night, all the catchers, except us and Shika, set off on the five-hundred-mile journey back to South Georgia. We had to wait with the factory overnight until the processing of the day's catch was completed, and the factory had enough steam to power its engines.

There was thick fog when we set off for Leith Harbour on the morning of Sunday 10th March 1940. However, in the early afternoon, it cleared into a grand day. On Monday, despite being under a clear sky, we were thrown about quite a lot because of a pretty rough sea. Tuesday was much the same, but we had the added interest of seeing some icebergs along the way. We eventually approached our destination between 9 and 10 p.m. Because of driving snow, and it being a pitch-black night, the factory took a long time to negotiate its entrance to the harbour.

I woke up about 7 a.m. on Wednesday morning. On looking through the porthole, I discovered that we were alongside at Stromness, taking on water. It was a fine morning. The second engineer and I walked along to an old pier and began fishing with the mate's hook and line. We had success right away. After breakfast, we were joined by the mate who was, in turn, followed by the chief. He caught the largest fish, which had a massive head.

Unfortunately, he thereafter lost our one and only hook. However, by this time, we had a full bucket of fish. They averaged about nine inches or so in length, some being a brownish colour and others pale green. In the afternoon, the gunner told me that there was a rumour that all the catchers were to be returning to the UK to be converted. Their new role - mine-sweeping duties.

Later in the day, the chief returned from a visit to the factory and said that the secretary had asked why I had not called for the mail. This was news to me, but, after our evening meal, I duly made my way over to New Sevilla. She was now moored alongside the Saluta which was lying at the pier where I collected the waiting mail. This consisted of a large mailbag plus a fair-sized box. After struggling with this load across Saluta's deck, I had to get the assistance of a deckhand to get it all down the gangplank. Next, it was onto a motor launch which conveyed me back across the bay to Sirra. On opening my letters, I noticed they had been written in November and, from the comments within, it was obviously expected that they would be in my possession before Christmas.

After returning the empty mailbag to Sevilla, I walked back along the shore where I met Mr Johnston at the Radio Equipment store. He informed me that it was almost certain that the catchers would indeed be going back to the UK. However, the full details were not yet known. Being small, the catcher vessels would obviously have to refuel more often. With the possibility of more frequent calls at various ports, this prospect began to appeal to me.

I enjoyed my return walk to Sirra. It was a grand day and felt quite warm compared to the ice fields. Later in the afternoon, I had a visit from the R/O from another catcher. He hinted that I would be filling the position of third R/O on the New Sevilla on the journey home. In fact, he had filled that position on the journey down, as I had similarly done on the Salvestria. It was clear that, for some unknown reason, he did not want to repeat the experience.

I spoke to Mr Johnston about this and his reply was that if all the catchers were required to go home, all the R/Os would obviously be required. In any case, I thought Sevilla could continue to work with two R/Os as at present. I could only wait and see what happened. I learned that there was to be a film show on shore tonight, so I returned later to see it. Unfortunately, I was late and only saw the latter half of 'Rose Marie', but I enjoyed the change of scenery. On my return, I found there was no heating on-board, and only poor lighting, which was due to a lack of steam.

On Friday, the mate gave me a haircut before I left to go ashore for a walk, where I met up with Robertson for a chat. As soon as I returned to the Sirra, I saw MacDonald's catcher, Sluga, arriving in the harbour. The Sluga had been fishing for the factory ship Sourabaya, which had arrived back earlier that day. I presumed that they had been further away than us when fishing had ceased. I boarded Sluga later in the evening and had a chat with MacDonald.

Again, I heard the rumour that the Sevilla was sailing out tomorrow, and the catchers were going alone.

On Sunday, it transpired that we were to go alongside the Sevilla, which was now anchored out in the harbour. At breakfast, the gunner, mate and steward were animated in their conversation, which was in their native tongue. Nevertheless, it became obvious to me that I was the topic of their conversation. When they had finished speaking, the steward gave me a strange look and said,

"Are you not going ashore, Sparks?

We will pick you up beside Sourabaya later."

I realised that this was a strong hint for me to make myself scarce. If I was to be asked for when we were alongside Sevilla, they could truthfully say I was not on-board. So, I promptly left to pay unannounced visits to Naismith as well as Arthur, the Cornishman.

Whilst on my way back to rejoin Sirra, I met Sevilla's R/O. He was clearly keen that I fill the position as his third R/O on Sevilla and asked if I had been transferred yet. I promptly replied that I had not and made it clear I had no intention of doing so if humanly possible. When I got back on-board Sirra, I was told that we had to take the Magistrate out to Sevilla for the purpose of signing-on extra crew. We remained alongside for two and a half hours, during which time I was hiding down in the engine room behind the boilers, being almost roasted alive!

After returning the Magistrate to shore, we were ordered to come straight back to Sevilla. So, once again, I made my way down to the boilers. Whilst hiding out, the second engineer came to update me. Mr Sprott, the first R/O, had asked to see me but they told him I was not on-board. However, the secretary had also arrived to speak to the gunner. It was then that I was told I had better go on-board Sevilla to see him.

I did so, and as expected, he wanted me to sign on. Maintaining my position of resistance, I eventually got out of it by saying that I had never been approached personally on the matter by Mr Sprott. All I knew about the proposal was through rumours circulating ashore. Alas, this reprieve proved to be temporary as the issue had started to move up the hierarchical chain. After a further trip ashore, I was summoned by the captain of the Sevilla who made it clear that I was to be the third R/O. I had to return ashore to the office, sign off the Sirra and sign on the New Sevilla. So, that was that!

As I arrived at the office, the Magistrate was sitting waiting for me. He looked at my papers and, looking up, said,

"So, you come from Perthshire?"

In reply, I asked if he knew Perthshire and was quite taken aback when he replied,

"Oh yes! I come from Pitlochry."

When I said that the early years of my life were spent in the nearby village of Kirkmichael, that certainly got him going. He ran through a list of names, including Dan

Menzies the joiner, Crichton the blacksmith, and others, but one name I was not acquainted with was someone called Davie Stewart. I think he was disappointed I knew nothing of this Davie, so I reminded him I had been only four years old when we left Kirkmichael. I had, however, kept up with the Menzies' who were next-door neighbours and very good to me. On leaving the office after the signings, the Magistrate, whose name I believe was Barlass, offered me his best wishes -

"I hope you have a good trip home."

Boarding Sirra for the last time, I was taken out to join the Flf (floating factory) New Sevilla. With a very heavy heart, I took leave of my very good friends on Sirra with whom I had become so close. As my case and belongings were being hoisted aboard my new 'home', the gunner, who I suspected had a good drink in him by this time, kept shaking my hand. He was at pains to tell me that he had done all he could in an effort to keep me on-board. In reply, I assured him I realised this fully, and thanked him for all he had done. I moved on to say farewell to the engineers and steward, who seemed equally sorry I was leaving them, and I felt honoured by that. After the long, slow climb up the rope-ladder to the deck of Sevilla, I turned and gave a last wave of the hand in salute to Sirra and friends.

Chapter 3 - SS New Sevilla

Fig.11 SS New Sevilla

Mr Sprott, the first R/O, was the first to greet me on Sevilla's deck. One of the other catcher R/Os helped with my large case and led me below decks. The steward then showed me to a room next to the officers' mess. The room, it transpired, was supposed to be used by two gunners, and was in complete contrast to the cabin I had shared on the trip down in Salvestria. I began to feel a bit better about where I had ended up now that the waiting and suspense were over. After what had become a busy last day on South Georgia, we sailed out of Leith Harbour shortly after my arrival on-board.

I then wondered if my hiding out, etc, had caused any delay in our departure, although thankfully, nobody ever mentioned it. A black-out was being enforced as I took my first watch at midnight. I was surprised to learn that no log was to be written up, being only a listening watch for any emergencies. It was also a surprise to learn that the Sevilla was, formerly, the White Star liner SS Runic. Similarly, its sister ship, Salvestria, was previously the SS Caernarvonshire. It was also revealed that our first port of call was to be Freetown in Sierra Leone.

My first watch was uneventful and I did not get up for breakfast, but on rising at 10 a.m., I found we were going 'dead-slow' because of thick fog and the presence of icebergs.

The weather remained bad and I was finishing my tea when the signal was raised for boat drill. Firstly, I was unaware to which boat I had been allocated and, secondly, I had not yet been given a lifejacket. Eventually, I found out that I was to report to 'number one' boat. The weather was good the following day with the sea quite smooth. Although it was a bit close inside, there was a nice breeze on deck. The good weather continued to prevail. On Thursday, our latitude was 36 degrees south which had us clear of the 'Roaring Forties'. When I came off watch at 4 a.m. on Saturday morning, I traversed the galley and found the former mate from the catcher MV Santa standing there with another man. The mate was called Maaren and the other was Watne. They were also on the midnight to 4 a.m. watch, had been able to get breakfast as soon as they came off watch, and said I should join them.

The day before, when Maaren had told me that Sunday's breakfast was to be ham and eggs, I thought he was joking. But true enough, on my arrival at their mess, there it was, and what a lovely sight and smell. It was marvellous being able to get breakfast so early. Otherwise, I would not have had anything to eat between 6 p.m. yesterday and 11:30 a.m. today. However, I did miss the porridge which I used to get on the catcher. Maaren looked in to see me during the afternoon watch. He took great delight in telling me that he had risen from his bunk at 8 a.m. to partake of a second breakfast which included grapefruit and cornflakes.

We had a very nice dinner today, and I was surprised when the captain ordered the steward to fetch a bottle of Dutch Gin to the table. The Whale Inspector and I were the only ones who did not partake. There was another surprise on the afternoon watch when my three o'clock cup of tea was accompanied by a sponge cake with cream and no less than five shortbread biscuits - such luxury! However, all was revealed when Watne later reminded me that it was Easter Sunday, hence the special treatment. The weather was nice again today with a slight but not cold breeze, however, it clouded over later.

At last, I got my lifejacket today from the mate. I also learned that most of the ship's crew have been on a four day holiday, which is apparently a Norwegian custom at this time of year. Peter, a crewman of small stature and wearing very baggy trousers, gave a solo performance on deck this afternoon. This involved balancing various articles, such as axes, iron stanchions and wooden planks, on his forehead, nose and chin. He balanced a long-handled brush on one raised foot, whilst hopping about the deck on the other. Following this, he turned somersaults and finally gave an involved demonstration of a bullfighter plying his craft in the bullring. With a handkerchief in one hand, he would wave to attract the 'invisible' bull, and with a stick in the other, he made thrusts at the imaginary animal. At the conclusion of his act, Peter simulated placing his foot upon the body of the downed animal to deliver the final *coup de grace*. This resulted in loud cheering from the large audience, who were then rewarded with two or three *encores*, before the 'actor' finally bowed to all sides and then left the 'stage'.

Over the next few days, the weather continued to improve and painting of the ship in battleship grey was in full swing. In addition, the bridge and the radio room were given a protective screen of sandbags in case of attack. During this time, we had been intercepting regular transmissions from Ascension Island of a coded message addressed to all British merchant ships. Unfortunately, we didn't yet have the codes necessary for translation. I was delighted to hear from the second R/O, Archie Turnbull, that on our return home, he would send me the negatives of his photographs taken during the fishing expedition, so I could get prints made from those I chose to have.

At the 4 a.m. breakfast, Maaren, Watne, Hansen (the third engineer) and I were receiving extra special attention from the night steward. We were offered a selection of peaches, cranberries, corn flakes and puffed rice. I then realised what I had been missing during the past five months or so.

On Saturday 30th March, we 'crossed the line' at 3 a.m. It turned out to be a very warm day and there was only a very slight swell on the sea. Later in the day, we saw our first ship since leaving Leith Harbour. It appeared to be a passenger ship and was sailing in the opposite direction. All going well, we expected to reach Freetown on Monday. In addition, orders were given that, as from that evening, blackout was to be even more strictly observed, including no smoking on deck.

Sunday was the hottest day so far, with the only breeze coming from the speed of the ship. It was being said that the two gunners wanted to leave the ship at Freetown. This was to attempt passage on a Mediterranean-bound vessel, and then a plane to Holland, if at all possible. Their objective was to avoid the now perilous North Sea Passage to Norway. However, it was thought to be a forlorn hope.

After our 4 a.m. breakfast on the first day of April, Maaren and I met up on deck. We realised we had reached the approaches to Freetown, as there were navigation lights close by. When I finally got to my bunk about 5 a.m., I thought how amazing it was to arrive, in pitch darkness, at two very small lights, having travelled some four thousand miles from South Georgia without sight of land. On wakening at 8 a.m. and looking through the porthole, I saw we were just entering the bay, so I decided to rise and get dressed.

From the deck, it seemed Freetown was situated on a sound, with an island lying off and parallel to the shore. There appeared to be two entrances to the bay; one main, large one and one small one, where there were quite a number of ships lying at anchor. Although it was slightly hazy along the shoreline, I could see that Freetown lay at the foot of a range of hills, with a scattering of houses situated on the slopes.

As soon as we had dropped anchor, the 'bumboats' arrived alongside. The first of these to arrive were small, single-seater canoes made out of hollowed tree trunks. The local native occupants begged for money and unwanted clothing. Amazingly, if a coin was thrown down, they dived quickly into the shark-infested water before resurfacing with it clenched between their teeth.

Larger canoes arrived with three or four occupants plus a large variety of goods and chattels. These comprised everything from monkeys, chickens, coconuts, bananas, limes, oranges, mangoes, raffia baskets, animal skins, horns, multi-coloured tablecloths and leather slippers to swords in leather scabbards. However, the monkeys were poor, pathetic creatures and the captain immediately issued orders that none were to be allowed on-board.

The locals actually preferred goods rather than money. When it was indicated that a deal might be done, a line, weighted with a banana or mango, was thrown up to the deck. This had a basket attached, into which you placed the items you wished to barter, before lowering it to the boat below. In my first deal, I disposed of an old jacket, trousers, pullover, waistcoat, underwear, soap, matches and cigarettes. This resulted in my receiving, after some detailed negotiations, loads of bananas, oranges, mangoes, two raffia baskets, slippers, a horn and a deerskin. Later, I received a huge bunch of bananas (about eighty in all) in exchange for a towel and a pair of socks.

Some of the locals were quaintly attired. One, in particular, did stand out with his fashion choice. Wearing a very English bowler hat, collar and tie, he had forgone the idea of a shirt but did sport a loincloth to complete his outfit. Another even wore a badly torn (ladies) floral frock! They did have a sufficient command of English to carry out trading, as well as singing. Two favourites seemed to be 'The Lambeth Walk' and, 'It ain't Gonna Rain No More'. When trading, they generally addressed you as 'Charlie' or 'Johnnie'. Their canoes were being regularly bailed out with the use of the husk of a coconut. Some of their larger canoes had names painted on the bow, one being called, 'Monday K. Amara' and another, 'Quick Penny'.

So-called bumboat trading was apparently not approved of by the local authorities. There were regular patrols by a launch in an effort to keep them away from vessels anchored in the bay. However, it was a bit farcical, as whenever the launch was sighted, the boats temporarily withdrew from the ship's side, only to return later.

I learned later that poor Peter, the lad who did the bullfighter act, had exchanged some clothes, including his good coat and a sheath knife, for a very miserable-looking monkey. Apparently, he had been desperate to have a monkey and had been enquiring of some members of the crew, long prior to our arrival, what they were likely to cost. Of course, he was not allowed to keep the monkey, but neither did he get his items returned.

Whilst writing up my diary in port, I was continually swatting flies which were becoming a real problem. However, not having a watch to do, I was hoping to get a decent night's sleep for once. We learned that two days prior to our arrival, the Coronda had left here in convoy. However, finding she had insufficient speed to keep up with the other ships, she had been forced to return to harbour. Nevertheless, she left again in a slower-moving convoy and was believed to be carrying our mail which had been written back in January. It seemed unlikely our letters would reach home much before ourselves.

The canoes were back again at an early hour, but orders had been given that we were not allowed to trade. The reason for this was that some of the messboys, having exhausted their stock of personal belongings, had been raiding the ship's stores. They had then proceeded to quietly trade goods through portholes below decks. In any case, it was very difficult to keep the canoes at bay. That was until my friend Maaren found a compromise solution.

One local lad in a single-seater canoe, who called himself 'Tellee Baby', was particularly popular with the crew due to his very commanding voice. Maaren had the bright idea of giving him the task of chasing the other boats away from the ship's side. This he succeeded in doing as efficiently as he did when diving for coins. By the end of the day, he returned ashore well-rewarded with money and clothing. No doubt he had already established an understanding with his fellow countrymen.

After coffee, I watched provisions being taken on-board, which proved to be an entertainment in itself. The 'babble' that accompanied this task was something quite unbelievable. It involved the local suppliers bawling at everyone else in their foreign tongue, which almost led to blows at times. Suddenly, in the midst of all of this, and whilst standing at the ship's rail, I heard further shouting. It was coming from elsewhere, and on turning around, I saw a canoe positioned off the side of the ship. The occupants of the canoe were, with much gesticulation, pointing towards our stern. I then heard 'shark!'

I immediately ran aft along the deck in the direction of the commotion. As I reached the stern, I heard a loud 'crack' which was caused by a rope breaking. It had been attached to the shark which was about to be pulled over the ship's rail onto the deck. However, it had now dropped back into the water.

Shortly afterwards, another shark was caught on the other side of the stern and was hauled in until its head was out of the water. The locals became terribly excited and canoes were arriving at speed from all directions. The occupants were all screaming instructions and advice on how to deal with it. Eventually, one of the bolder men in a large canoe offered to cut open the belly if the shark could be hauled further out of the water.

This being done, the volunteer approached slowly, making a tentative cut to the fin. He was complaining that his knife was too short and asked for a butcher's knife from the ship. With some suspicion as to motive, this request was not complied with, it being expected that the knife would never be seen again. Then, without warning, there was a loud 'splash'. The shark was now back in the water, and right in the middle of the encircling canoes!

The stalemate over the knife had somehow led to the hook becoming dislodged and complete pandemonium ensued. The occupants of the canoes were now frantically using their paddles to get away from the shark which had swallowed so much air it could not submerge. For one moment, it headed straight towards a large canoe, which it might have hit and capsized, but miraculously, this did not happen. After the initial panic had subsided, about seven or eight canoes began pursuing the shark. Alternately propelling their vessel with their paddles and then waving them in the air, the shouting and screaming continued throughout the whole proceedings. One man was seen to make a terrific swipe at the fish, but on missing it, he struck the side of his own canoe, breaking his paddle in two!

Meanwhile, a launch bringing the captain and two gunners back from shore then joined in the chase. One of the gunners managed on several occasions to get a grip on the quarry with a boathook but was forced to let go because of its tremendous strength. At one stage, it looked as if the launch would overturn in its efforts. Eventually, they were successful and finally secured their prey close to a Polish vessel, which had just arrived in the harbour.

After placing a noose around the shark's tail, the launch arrived at Sevilla with gunner Mikaelsen proudly standing on the bow and holding the rope with the shark in tow. The crewmen who had initially hooked the fish had already put a line down the slipway for it to be pulled up on deck. However, much to their dismay, the catch was duly presented back to the locals who immediately cut it up for themselves. They then disappeared as quickly as they had arrived. It was a fitting result to an impressive endeavour by all concerned. As someone safely looking down on the scene from a secure position, I have to admit it was one of the funniest (if not most dangerous) sights I had ever seen.

The Polish ship referred to in the shark saga turned out to be a troopship carrying French native soldiers bound for Marseilles. They wore khaki uniforms and red Fez hats, and it did appear that the ship was quite overcrowded.

When the captain returned on-board, he informed us we would not be leaving before Sunday. He also said the two gunners had not been successful in their request to return to Norway via France and Holland. This, of course, was not a surprise.

Wednesday began dull and close, but improved as the day wore on. The mate spent most of the day chasing away bumboats with the aid of a water hose, but all to no avail. A local man of more superior appearance arrived this afternoon in a rowing boat, offering horn-ware, knives and spears for sale. I succumbed and bought a short-handled spear decoratively-adorned with leather and deerskin.

Another shark was caught today and cut up on deck. One chap tried to remove the backbone but had to give up the task. Several teeth were removed and, on investigation, I found they were surprisingly small. Nevertheless, they were still razor-sharp, resembling the teeth in a saw. It was pointed out to me that the teeth were not set in a jawbone, but gristle. The heart had also been taken out and placed in a life-raft, where it seemed to continue pumping.

The following day was very warm, and, during the evening, we saw the factory ship, Sourabaya, arriving in harbour to join us. The next morning also saw the arrival of Salvestria to join the waiting fleet of Salvesen ships. The warm weather continued, and in the afternoon a large number of canoes came out to fish with nets. The locals kept hauling in the nets with apparent non-stop success. The sight of the silver-coloured fish made quite a spectacle. The many sailing boats which ply between the mainland and island also make a fine sight. They are basically normal rowing boats, but also equipped with a large three-cornered sail which gives them quite a good turn of speed.

Sourabaya began refuelling this afternoon, and a few hours later, another tanker came alongside for the same purpose. She was a Fleet Reserve ship and had on-board a great assortment of monkeys, parrots, canaries and other birds. There were two very amusing monkeys with white noses that made them look very much like kittens.

At an evening concert on deck, Maaren told me that he and Henson had, for the past two nights, been able to acquire a late snack of peaches and cornflakes. They promised to come and wake me if they were still up that night. One might think I was being starved. Maaren was a very interesting man, and full of humour. He had worked in America for a number of years and told tales of his adventures there, as well as his home in Norway. He was quite a lad, and I enjoyed his company.

Captain Jamieson from the Salvestria came on-board to tell us they would not be sailing for another week and asked if we could oblige by giving two of his gunners passage home. This was agreed to, but it meant I had to vacate my spacious cabin. My move was to a two-berth cabin situated close to the saloon and was occupied by a young man called Schianders who, I was led to understand, was related to a branch of the Salvesen family. As to his position on-board, I was not quite sure, although I believed he helped in the secretary's office. He was a well-spoken but quiet young man. Although I did not see a great deal of him due to my watches, we did seem to get on quite well together.

We sailed from the bay at 5:15 a.m. on Sunday in a convoy of seventeen ships escorted by an Armed Merchantman vessel. We were arranged in line-abreast formation, comprising two lines of six, and one of five at the rear. Sourabaya and ourselves occupied the third and fourth positions in the second line, and therefore, in the middle of the convoy. This was presumably done because we were carrying the most valuable cargoes. I was told, in strict secrecy, that our destination was London.

Monday was a fine day but with a cooler breeze. One ship, which had been falling behind the previous night, was not to be seen. Another was also lagging. A message was issued by the Commodore stating the standard of black-out on all ships was, *'not good enough!'*. This resulted in more restrictions being imposed on-board Sevilla. The Norwegians were quite alarmed when they heard news reports saying mines had been laid in Norwegian waters.

On Tuesday, the two laggard vessels had resumed their positions in the convoy which, I imagine, would have been to their great relief. I had a rare visit from the captain before dinner. I got the feeling he was perhaps a little apprehensive of how I had accepted my enforced move to another cabin. He opened the conversation by saying,

"You are much better here than in a catcher, eh?

Anyway, we should be home at least a week before them."

In the evening, whilst at supper in the saloon, we heard the news of the invasion of Norway. As might be expected, this had an 'electric' effect on the Norwegians, causing a loud babble to ensue. Full details were not immediately available, however, a news-sheet was to be produced nearer to midnight. From what I could gather, Britain was more than likely to be blamed for allowing the invasion to occur!

The following day, there was a great demand for more news and, as predicted, many of the Norwegians were already blaming Britain for this 'disaster'. On coming off watch at 4 a.m. on Thursday, I was surprised to see a large passenger liner all lit-up. It was thought to be Italian. On Friday, the convoy was joined by another ship. It was pleasing to hear on the news that a large minefield had been laid, which had the effect of closing off the Baltic Sea.

Saturday was a fine day and quiet, at least until 7:30 p.m. I was walking on deck prior to going to my bunk when I was suddenly startled by hearing a ship's 'bummer' being sounded. It turned out to be from the Vice Commodore's vessel, situated on the extreme starboard end of the first line of ships in the convoy. This was then repeated by the Commodore's ship which also fired off a green-coloured Very Light into the sky. Continuing to observe, I saw the two outside ships in the rear convoy line were now showing their navigation lights. At that moment, one of the mates came along and told me the reason for the disturbance. This was to signal a change of course for the convoy.

The obvious question was, *who all knew about this?* Certainly not I, nor our non-watch passengers, who, every night, occupied most of the afterdeck. There was quite a panic raised. Those who were not already wearing life jackets, rushed below decks to fetch them amid shouts of,

"To the lifeboats!".

This duly wakened others from their bunks to add to the commotion. I could not help thinking to myself, '*What would it be like if it was the real thing?*' On Sunday evening, this point was again made just as the sun was setting. Smoke from a ship was sighted directly in the path of the sun. Our escort turned off in their direction, only to turn back as the ship had disappeared.

Next day, a large school of porpoises came close alongside the ship and passed directly across our bow. The following day, it was becoming much colder. At this time, we were on a zig-zagging course - a tactic designed to hinder any possible U-boat attack. We caught up with a small trawler-type vessel which sent a signal to the escort vessel having moved off slightly from the convoy. Shortly afterwards, we sighted what appeared to be some kind of vessel which led to a great deal of speculation as to exactly what it was. In fact, it turned out to be the stern half of a tanker. It had obviously been broken off by either a mine or a torpedo, and the trawler was apparently keeping watch over it.

The weather continued to deteriorate over the next few days and we kept zig-zagging on occasion. Sunday was misty with a rough sea and a strong wind blowing. Two naval destroyers joined us, giving welcome extra protection, along with a large RAF seaplane which was circling the convoy during the afternoon. Later in the evening, the convoy split up. Eleven ships, including Sourabaya, headed for the west coast with one destroyer, whilst we, along with five others and the second destroyer, were destined for the English Channel. On the next day, the sea was calmer with us now being clear of the Bay of Biscay. The seaplane continued patrolling overhead and we were engaged in even more zig-zagging.

It was a dull, rainy and foggy day when we dropped anchor at Plymouth at 1:30 p.m. on the 23rd of April. Amongst the many ships at anchor, we were surprised to see the Coronda, which we later learned had only arrived the previous day. Their slow passage had been due to her having lost two blades from her propeller. I was pleased to hear that our mail, which she had been carrying, had been forwarded earlier from Freetown. We were expected to be lying here for several days. An anti-magnetic (anti-mine) device was to be fitted around the ship. This took the form of electric cables attached to the sides to prevent the hull from attracting German magnetic mines.

The fog persisted until the following morning, but improved during the afternoon, although it remained cold. I was speaking to a lad on deck this evening, and he asked if I had seen the 'man on horseback' cut into the turf above the cliffs. I had not but recalled learning about it during my school days. Coronda left this morning and we heard our departure would probably be on Friday.

On Thursday, a naval team fitted the ship with the temporary 'degaussing' (DG) device, allowing us to leave as planned the following afternoon. Unfortunately, we had to return to harbour when the DG cables were found to have a problem. We lifted anchor again on Saturday but spent some time testing the DG equipment. We also adjusted compasses before finally sailing on our way in mid-afternoon. The fog was coming down and making our progress very slow, and this continued on Sunday. We had to stop engines between 3 and 4 p.m., whilst blowing our bummer at frequent intervals.

Later, I was preparing to go to my bunk and standing with only my trousers on when I heard the sound of another ship's bummer. Realising it must be very close by, this was confirmed when there was a great 'shudder'. I was sure there had been a collision. Schianders came rushing in to collect his life jacket and confirmed my suspicion. I quickly put on a jersey and my shoes and made my way on deck. I was just in time to see the bows of a ship slowly drawing away from our stern on the port side. The deck was crowded with life-jacketed figures as I made my way to the stern. We had been hit just to the side of the whale slipway. It was a fascinating sight to witness the damage that had been caused. It looked for all the world like a side of cheese with a large wedge cut out. On one side of the gaping 'wedge' could be seen the remains of a lower deck toilet. I for one would not have wished to be seated there when the collision occurred!

The bow of the colliding ship had cut into us for a depth of ten to twelve feet and into a passageway below decks. One could see nothing except twisted metal and splintered planks of wood from the decks. The newly-fitted DG cables were cut right through and it was fortunate there had been no outbreak of fire. A destroyer soon appeared on the scene and led the offending vessel away. It appeared to be a fairly large ship, but I was unable to make out her name.

After roughly half an hour or so, I returned to my cabin and bunk to try to get some sleep prior to taking my usual watch at midnight. At the end of my watch, I found the fog had lifted somewhat, and I could see navigation lights on the many ships around us. After I had taken my usual breakfast, I found the fog had come down once more, but decided to go along and have another look at the damage. I found the chief engineer and Danny, the electrician, busily engaged in repairing the DG cables, which they were confident of successfully completing very shortly.

We were moving towards Devonport very slowly, in company with other ships, and quite close together.

This was due to the continuing fog, which lifted and fell intermittently throughout the day. At about 4:45 p.m., we were quite close to the cliffs, when we had to pass between two buoys whilst a submarine was keeping guard. At the same time, two large bomber aircraft were continually circling above us.

There were large numbers of birds flitting about the deck today; mainly swallows or sand-martins. The ship's cats kept stalking them, but fortunately, with little success. A pilot came on-board at night, but the next day the fog was so bad that we remained stationary all day.

On the morning of the first day of May, we were cleared to proceed. Although the fog persisted, we had, in any case, to wait for the tide turning at 3 p.m. It was after 4 p.m. when we eventually set off as the fog had cleared slightly. We hoped it would not return, as we were said to be in the most dangerous area for attack. We could see barrage balloons attached to vessels at the mouth of the Thames, which were intended to prevent air attacks by low-flying aircraft. We anchored off Thames Haven at 7:30 p.m. and I was pleased when Second R/O Archie Turnbull informed me I did not have to take the midnight watch.

Next day, we moved alongside in the early afternoon and the discharging of our cargo commenced immediately. Archie was told by Mr Sprott to stand-by the ship for a number of days. I, on the other hand, was able to sign-off at 4:30 p.m. but left behind the antelope skin which I had purchased in Freetown. I did not have the space to pack it, and to be honest, it didn't seem quite as attractive as when initially acquired.

After saying my goodbyes, I headed for the dock gates. Double-decker buses were waiting at the dock to transport myself and others directly to King's Cross Station. Lorries had been contracted to take our luggage. We arrived at the station at 8:30 p.m. After getting our tickets and attending to our baggage, a group of us decided to go for a meal at a top hotel. The train north was not due to leave until 10:30 p.m. There were seven or eight of us in the group, including Doctor Wardle, Mr Sprott and myself. I do not recall the names of the others, nor the name of the chosen hotel, but I certainly remember the reception we received.

Whether it was our appearance after some six and a half months at sea, or perhaps the lingering smell of whale oil, I do not know. The restaurant waitress who approached certainly had the knack of making us feel out of place. Despite being dressed in naval uniform, she seemed very reluctant to even show us to a table. Her crowning glory, however, came after she received our simple order for *mixed grills all round* when she said, in a steely voice,

"Would you pay now?!"

She was somewhat taken aback at the response this produced when, in no uncertain terms, we were immediately back on our feet, ready to walk out. However, peace was finally restored when we were invited to re-take our seats, with due apologies. We again sat down to enjoy our mixed grills. This was my first visit to London, and I must admit, I was not sorry to leave it.

The train was very busy with a large contingent of British Expeditionary Force (BEF) soldiers going on home leave. Tired though I was, the noise completely eliminated any possibility of sleeping. I was more than pleased to be able to get a cup of tea when we stopped at Newcastle. It was 7:15 a.m. on Friday when we arrived in Edinburgh. After taking leave of the others, Mr Sprott and I had a coffee before making our way down to Christian Salvesen's offices in Bernard Street, Leith.

We found out we had arrived too early and the offices were not yet open, so we retired to a small café for tea and rolls. Returning once more, we successfully collected our wages up to date. However, this did not include our oil bonus. The amount due could not be determined until the oil had been sold, which could take a few months. We learned at the office that some of the factory ships, including the New Sevilla, were to go on the crude-oil tanker trade, and would be likely to employ only two radio officers instead of three.

After taking leave of Mr Sprott, I caught the 10:05 a.m. train to Perth, arriving there an hour and a half later. As my parents did not have a telephone at this time, I phoned the garage adjacent to my home, and asked Mrs Stuart, the owner's wife, if she would let my parents know I was back and would catch the first bus home. I stepped off the bus at 12:30 p.m. to the warmest of welcomes and a joyful reunion after six and a half months' absence. It was good to be home.

(Editor's Note: More than a decade after the author's passing in 2000, an elderly resident of Crieff discovered a newspaper dated Saturday 11ᵗʰ May 1940, lining a drawer in her home. Recognising the youthful face of the author, she commented to her daughter, who, in turn, knew the author's younger son (Iain), and the 'souvenir' was duly passed on.

Fig.12 People's Journal 11 May 1940 Author Story

The People's Journal story, "U-Boat Attack on Convoy: Thrills in a Catcher", is in part replicated as printed below.

'THRILLS *of an attempted U-boat attack on a convoy*

and chasing whales at 16 knots an hour in rough seas!
These are among the experiences of Mr Alex. Anderson, elder son
of Mr J.B. Anderson, school-master, Methven, who is home after
a six months' voyage. When he rounded off his education at Perth
Academy Mr Anderson decided to become a wireless operator. The
Mercantile Marine was his goal, and when he got his 'ticket' he
was lucky enough to get one of the most adventurous jobs in the
world.

He sailed in October for the colourful whaling station at South
Georgia as 'Sparks' aboard one the world's strangest craft, a
floating factory ship specially designed for handling whales.'

'Convoy Thrill – *Some of the ships in the convoy were*
harassed by U-boats, but the Nazis missed the factory ship. The
journey out was uneventful, said Anderson and the ship only
made one landfall for the sake of refuelling, But, soon after South
Georgia was reached it was a case of 'action stations'.'

'Mr Anderson was transferred to one of a fleet of 'catcher'
craft, fast and manoeuvrable boats that hunt down the whales
in the wide-open spaces of the South Atlantic, often far into the
Antarctic.'

'My job is then to flash messages to the base and the floating
factory, on which I travelled out from this country.'

'Whales are very much worthwhile catching. They are full of
the most valuable oils and fats.'

Part II

North Atlantic convoys
(1940 – 1945)

Fig. 13 North Atlantic convoy with Aerial Support

"The only thing that ever really frightened me during the war was the U-boat peril."

(Winston Churchill, Their Finest Hour
(London: Cassell, 1949), 529.)

Chapter 4 – SS Peder Bogen

Fig.14 – SS Peder Bogen

After returning from Christian Salvesen's Whaling Expedition on 3rd May 1940, I was invited to join another of their fleet as second R/O. This was the SS Peder Bogen, a former Norwegian vessel of 7,363 net tonnage, which was lying at South Shields.

Coming under the Military Charter, I was now *de-facto* RN personnel. Another specific security factor of the time, which would affect me later on, was that all communications on-board foreign-registered vessels had to be under the control of British R/Os.

I joined the Peder Bogen on Thursday 23rd March and was surprised to find that she was still in dry dock.

However, with the captain's permission, I returned home for the weekend. Re-joining the ship on Tuesday coincided with the sad announcement of Belgium's capitulation. As it happened, we didn't actually sail from the Tyne until 30th May. Acting as Commodore ship, we led a small convoy of ships to Southend where we joined another convoy already waiting there.

We had been destined to go to Southampton for bunkers, but this was cancelled and we received fresh orders to proceed to Falmouth. At this time, the fighting at Dunkirk was going on. Hanging over the French coast was a huge pall of black smoke. We lay at Falmouth for about a week but were only allowed ashore on two occasions. The weather at the time was lovely, and we eventually left there in convoy with only two other ships and a naval escort. However, the escort left us after only one day. We were, once again, on our own.

Thankfully without incident, and in perfect weather all the way, we reached our destination at the island of Aruba in the Dutch West Indies on Monday 24th June 1940. After a visit ashore, I was surprised to hear the strains of a violin emanating from the captain's cabin. It transpired Captain Smith was no mean player, and I really enjoyed listening to his recital of Scottish airs and light classics. One piece I particularly liked was called The Isle of May. The performances were by no means regular occurrences, but they always gave me great pleasure. With our oil cargo safely on-board, we left on 26th June for Bermuda, and during this time, we learned of France's capitulation.

We arrived in Bermuda on July 2nd. Despite sailing out in convoy again the next morning, we were recalled back to Bermuda later the same day. On returning, we found to our surprise that Salvesen's whaling factory ship, Salvestria, was also lying in the bay. This, of course, was the first ship on which I had sailed to South Georgia for the 1939-40 whaling season. Captain Jamieson was still in command and he, together with two or three officers, came aboard Peder Bogen for a visit.

We learned they were to be sailing before us, and it was arranged for us to transfer an engineer, whom we had taken on-board in Aruba, back to Salvestria. He was described as a DBS (Distressed British Seaman). This could mean either he had missed the ship's sailing, or he was a survivor from a ship sunk by enemy action. However, the officers were not very keen to take the man off our hands. One said they did not want a *'Jonah'* on-board and another stated they *'so far, had never had any excitement'*, obviously hoping for that to continue. Little did they know what lay ahead for them.

We later learned that, after crossing the Atlantic safely and entering the Firth of Forth, the Salvestria had been sunk by an enemy mine. This was, of course, devastating news. What I did not know then was that this story would again be raised in the most unexpected of situations.

After the war (late 1940s), when I was staying with my parents and sister at Fowlis Wester, near Crieff in Perthshire, a local farmer called on us one evening. In the course of conversation, he mentioned being previously admitted to Edinburgh Infirmary, when one of his fellow patients had told him an extraordinary tale. This patient had been the captain of a ship which had sunk in the Forth. As the ship was sinking fast, he had to leave the ship's papers and his gold watch in the safe. There was, however, a happy ending to his story. A diver had been sent down and had successfully retrieved the ship's papers along with the gold watch. Amazingly, the watch still worked, none the worse for its submersion.

His story related, the farmer concluded rhetorically,

"I wish I could remember the man's name. All I know is, he was a Shetlander."

"Captain Jamieson," I replied.

The farmer swung round,

"That's right!" he shouted. *"How on earth did you know that?"*

We lay at anchor in Bermuda Bay for the whole month of July. The weather was beautiful, but no shore leave was allowed. However, the captain had a 'makeshift' canvas swimming pool erected on deck which provided a welcome relief for the crew.

Such simple pleasures were greatly appreciated but dangers were never far away. Sadly, we had a tragic accident on-board, as a result of which our third engineer was killed. He had been checking and adjusting the ship's steering gear mechanism (which controlled the rudder) at the stern of the ship when it occurred and it was ages before help arrived from the shore, but sadly, he was already gone. His body was taken ashore, covered by the Red Ensign, and he was buried there. Unfortunately, only three representatives from the ship were allowed to attend the burial.

Fig.15 Canvas Swimming Pool on SS Peder Bogen

On the last day of July, we set off for home, sailing up the North American coast in convoy. We eventually joined up with another convoy from Halifax, NS, to make the North Atlantic crossing. It was about this time that

I developed a swelling on the left side of my face. Centred about my top lip, it had steadily got worse. Captain Smith took a look at it but returned to his cabin to study a medical book. When he returned, he had a worried look on his face, and said he was unable to find any diagnosis of the condition. I was told to go to my bunk right away and stay there. When I asked, *"What about my shifts on watch?"* he replied,

"Never mind about that. Snowy will have to do it."

Snowy was the nickname of the first R/O, so-called by his very regular references to times spent in the Snowy River area of Australia, his home country. As we had no third R/O on-board at this time, Snowy was anything but pleased to do extra watches. Not that I heard this from him personally because, during the four or five days when I was confined to my bunk, he never visited once. In fact, he barely spoke to me for the rest of the voyage. My face was pretty badly swollen and distorted on the left side until about the third day when the ulcer (for this is what it became) suddenly burst on the inside of my lip. It was a great relief to me, it must be said. Not least for the fact that it stopped unsolicited visits from other crew members wanting to have a look at my hideous visage.

The weather was pretty bad all the way across the North Atlantic. This wasn't such a bad thing in that it lessened the chances of enemy action, and so it proved. We got sight of the Scottish coast as we sailed south on our way to Liverpool, where we discharged our cargo of oil. As we were alongside for about four days, it meant we were able to get ashore. However, we then had to move into the river where we lay for nearly three weeks. I do not have a record of precise dates, but within the first one or two weeks there, we witnessed a series of almost nightly air-raids on the city. Being in the river, it seemed as if we were in the middle of it. This left us feeling very vulnerable, especially with no defences on-board.

It was quite an experience, and at the same time, frightening to witness this first-hand. The sky was lit up with explosions and subsequent fires. There was a thunderous noise from the bomber aircraft passing overhead, coupled with the firing of anti-aircraft guns from the nearby shore defences. One expected that we would be hit at any minute.

In fact, in the morning, the deck was littered with bomb shrapnel. Towards the end of the second week, we were instructed to be ready to leave the following morning early. As a result, our assigned pilot came on-board the evening before. However, the DG anti-magnetic mine cables, which surrounded the outside of the ship's hull, burst into flames during the night. It was several days before workmen could complete the repairs.

On Thursday, 12th September, the day prior to our fated scheduled departure from Liverpool, I attended the usual pre-sailing conference. This was held at HMS Eaglet, the RN (Royal Navy) Shore Station. The naval telegraphist who presided said he would be on-board the SS City of

Benares, which would be the Commodore ship of the convoy. He then added,

"I have to tell you, it will be my thirteenth ship and my thirteenth crossing of the North Atlantic, and I don't have to tell you what follows!"

There was an immediate roar of laughter from the assembled gathering who were, of course, well aware the next day was Friday the 13th. Once again, little did everyone know the evil that lay ahead.

The following day, we did not get our intended early departure. Enemy bombers were over during the night, and the Port was closed until the entrance channel had been swept clear of mines. It was evening before we were able to sail. On Sunday, I heard a distress call from the SS Coronda, saying she was being attacked by a plane. The Coronda was another Salvesen ship, and well-known to me. She had been used as a supply ship during the earlier whaling season. We later learned she was on her way home from Iceland with a cargo of fish oil and had been hit aft by a bomb. Sadly, despite managing to reach port safely, twenty-one crewmen were reported missing. I understand it was Coronda's third war, having also been used as a troopship during the Boer War.

Three days later, our destroyer escort left us. Whether it was simply to return home alone or to escort an incoming convoy, we did not know. By this time, we were aware that the Commodore vessel, City of Benares, was carrying a lot of children as passengers. As we were abreast of her, on her port side, in the second line of ships, we had seen the children happily playing on deck.

About 10:15 p.m. the same night, I was rudely awakened from my bunk by the second steward with grim news. The Benares had been torpedoed. I hurriedly dressed, grabbed my life jacket and rushed to the radio room, where I learned a second ship had also been hit. Going out on deck, I could see the two stricken ships. Both were now lit up with many lights but, soon afterwards, the lights of one completely disappeared!

After being hit, the City of Benares, as the Commodore vessel, had fired a distress signal rocket. This meant that all ships were now on their own and had to make their escape separately, and as quickly as they could. Weather-wise, it was not a good night, with driving rain, sleet and snow. The sea was pretty rough and there was a strong wind. Only very occasionally was there a glimmer of the moon to be seen through the clouds.

Naturally, all our thoughts centred on the welfare of the children and crew taking to life-boats, some six hundred miles out in the North Atlantic, and under such dreadful conditions. For us, this was made even more tragic by the fact that we (Peder Bogen) had been delegated to act as the rescue ship for such an event. However, there was a strict proviso that this duty was only to be carried out, *'when naval escort ships were in attendance'*!

It was reported later that there were four hundred and six persons on-board the City of Benares, one hundred of whom were children being evacuated to Canada. Only one hundred and sixty-one survived, including only nineteen children. I couldn't help wondering if the telegraphist from the pre-departure conference survived.

Shortly after we dispersed from the convoy, a surfaced U-boat was seen from the bridge. It was approaching from astern, so we fired off several shells in its direction. It disappeared temporarily, before being seen again about 2 a.m., then finally disappearing for good. The following afternoon, another ship was sunk in the same area. Having witnessed this dreadful scene, it was brought even closer to home on my return. Incredibly, I learned that a young girl, Joyce Keay, from my own village, had been one of the child evacuees aboard the Benares. Thankfully, she was one of the survivors and I believe still lives in the Vancouver area of Canada.

It was only a week later when I overheard another distress signal from a ship well-known to me. The New Sevilla reported it had been torpedoed off Inishtrahull, Donegal, on Ireland's northern coast. This was Salvesen's whaling factory ship on which I had served as third R/O on its journey back from the Antarctic. Fortunately, and despite her damage, the Sevilla managed to reach port. However, the U-boat wolf-packs did not let up. The following day, another three ships were also torpedoed in the same area.

On Wednesday 2nd October, we arrived back at the island of Aruba in the Dutch West Indies. We learned that a detachment of the Cameron Highlanders was stationed there as a Defence Force to protect the highly precious oil which these islands supplied. After loading our cargo of oil, we left Aruba on the following Friday afternoon and headed north for Bermuda. During the night of Saturday into Sunday, we experienced the most amazing and violent electrical storms. There was thunder and lightning accompanied by torrential rain. The flashes lit up the ship and the sky as if it was daylight. When the ship's mast was struck by lightning, the noise of the 'bang' was unbelievable. In fact, the mate and steward, who had been in their bunks, came running to the bridge believing we were under attack!

It was a week later when, on a lovely day with a calm sea, it was decided we should have firing practice with our deck gun. The target was a large empty oil drum that had a stick with a white flag attached. The drum contained sufficient ballast to ensure it would continue to float upright. Being very heavy as a result, the drum had to be lowered over the ship's side with the aid of a crane. In addition, the drum had two thick strengthening bands around it.

The first mate was supervising the lowering along with the chief engineer when suddenly, there was a loud cry of pain. The mate was then seen 'dancing' about the deck on one leg whilst holding the other. It transpired his foot had been sticking slightly over the ship's side and had been caught by one of the strengthening bands on the drum as it descended. The seam of the mate's shoe-cap had burst open and was bent back, so that his toes ended up lying on top of the cap and, sadly, part of his big toe was torn off. Regretfully, those of us who were looking down on the incident from the boat-deck did not realise the severity of the injury at the time. I have to confess that when the mate was dancing and yelling, I (shamefully) took part in the ensuing communal laughter at his antics with my fellow onlookers.

Two days later, we reached Bermuda, as the Sourabaya, another of the company's ships, was leaving for Halifax, NS. The mate was able to get some medical attention for his injured foot, but, as usual, we got no shore leave. We left again on Monday and had good weather for the first two days. However, it became rough later on and one of our lifeboats was smashed. Five or six days later, we joined a convoy from Halifax, and the weather became progressively worse. This eventually resulted in the convoy becoming scattered because of dense fog. The convoy was not completely reformed until Sunday 27th October. On the previous day, we had intercepted a distress signal from the Liner, SS Empress of Britain, stating she had come under attack by enemy aircraft.

On Monday, we were met by naval escort ships, including one of the old four-funnelled destroyers that America had agreed to supply for the protection of Atlantic shipping. On the following night, we became separated from the convoy in terrible seas. During this time, we heard a message from a Dutch ship saying she was taking on water and sinking. On Wednesday, we met up with five of the other ships and an American destroyer. Later, we heard on the news that four ships had run aground on Rattray Head, Aberdeenshire, on Scotland's northeast coast.

We eventually dropped anchor in the River Clyde, near Glasgow, on the first day of November. On Monday, I enquired of the captain if there was any chance of getting home, but he said it was not possible until the ship had been given Customs clearance. The following afternoon, I was lying on my bunk when the second mate dashed in to tell me the captain had returned from shore, and his transfer boat would return in half an hour, at 4:30 p.m., to take off any crew with permission to go on leave. It was some rush for me, but I made it. The chief mate was also going home. Although in full uniform, his injured foot was still heavily bandaged and resting on the sole of a slipper. To be able to carry his case, he required the use of a stick to aid his walking.

Later, we were standing together on the station platform waiting for a train to Glasgow. I saw two elderly ladies standing close-by and looking in our direction with greatly concerned expressions. They were talking quietly but were quite animated in their conversation. I could just imagine them recounting later to their friends about the poor naval officer who had presumably been wounded in battle. There would, of course, be no clarification of the 'enemy', on this occasion, being a friendly oil drum. After arriving in Glasgow, I had to wait several hours before getting a train to Perth and it was after midnight before I arrived there. I then had to wait for a taxi, with the result that it was 1:15 a.m. before I was home.

After twelve days at home, I reported back to the ship on Monday 18th November. We sailed from the Clyde the following day, bound for Liverpool with a replacement chief mate and, for the first time, a third R/O. The weather became very rough during my watch and I stood up to see an extremely high wall of water coming at us, head-on. It hit us with a great shudder and the main deck, being low in the water because of our full cargo, was completely awash. When I returned to my cabin at the end of my watch, I was horrified to find it too was completely awash, with some things floating about the floor, and my bunk saturated. I had, of course, left a forward-facing porthole open!

We arrived at the Liverpool Bar on Thursday and lay there until Sunday when we proceeded up-river. We transferred some of our cargo to another ship there before returning to lie again at the Bar. On Tuesday we again sailed up-river, but this time, continued through the Manchester ship canal to Stanlow where we berthed. I was fortunate to get a further two weeks' leave.

When I returned to the ship on December 12th, it was now lying at Bromborough Dock. By mistake, I had carried on to Manchester on the train. When I eventually reached

Liverpool, I couldn't get a taxi to take me across the river to Bromborough, but did manage to get on the ferry boat. On reaching the other side, I was directed to a bus where I asked the Conductor to let me off at Bromborough Dock, which he did. Unfortunately, however, it turned out to be the wrong entrance. I then walked and walked without seeing anyone to direct me, before I managed to hail a 'pug' engine which was hauling trucks through the docks. I was very happy to accept the invitation to complete my journey on the footplate of this strange but welcome form of transport. On boarding the ship, I found almost everybody was ashore apart from the mate. He did not endear himself to me when he said,

"Are you back already? You could have had another week!"

Our new Master, Captain Dawson, attended a preliminary conference at which His Majesty the King was also present. We then sailed in convoy on the morning of Friday, December 20th. That night, as well as the following night, Liverpool was the main air raid objective of the enemy. On Sunday, a cabin boy collapsed with sea-sickness and on the following day, our escorting destroyers left us in the afternoon. This led to the convoy breaking up at around 5 p.m. when our position was 55.5 N, 17.5 W. Some of the crew were unhappy at escorts leaving us so soon, somewhat maliciously suggesting they were making sure 'they would get home for Christmas'. On Christmas Eve, decorations were being put up in the saloon.

On Christmas Day 1940, our position was 53N, 26W with the weather deteriorating in a heavy sea. The cabin boy was in his bunk again and unable to do his duties. I heard a distress signal from a ship to the northeast of us, saying she was being hit by gunfire from a surfaced submarine. We also heard the King's message to the Armed Forces today. Two days later, we were still experiencing bad weather and the ship's cat, Gertie, who had not been seen all day, was feared lost overboard. However, that night, when the mate pulled out a drawer below his bunk, its 'resurrection' was complete.

Hogmanay 1940 - our position was 38.59N, 43.28W, and it was not such a bad day. That night, over the radio, I heard Big Ben signalling the beginning of the New Year. On New Year's Day 1941, I had a glass of Port wine and shortbread to celebrate along with the second mate. At night, I was surprised to hear the Home BBC Radio Station broadcast loud and clear at a distance of two thousand, three hundred miles!

2nd January 1941 - I turned twenty-one years old today. The only celebratory activity was having my hair cut by the second mate. The ship's engine was stopped for a short period during the day, not on my behalf, but to enable minor repairs to be made. Saturday was the first good day of the voyage weather-wise, and I was able to have a spell lying out in the sunshine. A test shot was fired from our gun at a floating smoke target. The aim was good but the performance of the target was not so good. Sunday was another grand day and, on Monday, the sunrise was beautiful and the sea was like a sheet of glass. On Wednesday, we saw a large sailing ship some distance away and during the night, we entered the Caribbean.

On Tuesday evening, some of the crew were relaxing on deck and generally fooling around. The cabin boy joined us after apparently making a remarkable recovery from his long-lasting sea-sickness. One of the crew brought out a mop with a metal strainer tied to the end of the handle and, calling the boy forward, he handed it to him. Saying it was a special ship's microphone, he told the boy he could send a message to his family at home. Entering into the spirit, and being reminded he would have to speak loudly because of the distance from home, the boy pressed his lips close to the makeshift 'microphone' and roared out,

"Can you hear me, Dad?"

In the slight pause that followed, the second steward shouted out,

"Yes!"

And all the audience simultaneously exploded in laughter. Thus, the cabin boy got well and truly back into the good books of his shipmates, and a very happy evening ensued.

At 4 a.m. on Friday, we could see the glare in the sky from the lights of the island of Curaçao. Later, around 10:30 a.m., we sailed (literally) through the town via a floating bridge. This linked the two sections of the town with the harbour and its oil storage area beyond. However, we did not go alongside until the next day to discharge our water ballast and refill with oil. We were also allowed ashore, and again on Sunday, when I managed to take some photographs. We left the port between 7 and 8 a.m. on Monday, but without one seaman who had failed to re-join the ship. Later that day, we saw what appeared to be a very large waterspout emanating from the sea.

Two days later, we passed through the Mona Passage between Puerto Rico and Santo Domingo at 4 a.m. About one hour later, we passed an American passenger liner all lit up, which was an unusual sight for us. Whilst at dinner on Friday, the second mate came into the saloon and said a ship was making towards us on the port bow at quite a good speed. We altered course to port but she did not alter accordingly, so we resumed our prior course. She was passing quite close to us, so the captain ordered the Red Ensign to be hoisted, whereby the ship responded with the Dutch flag. On Saturday night, we neared Bermuda in fog so did not drop anchor there until the following day. We left again on Tuesday 21st January and experienced bad weather conditions for the next two or three days. During this time, the cabin boy returned to his bunk again, however, on being threatened that his wages would be stopped, he was out again the next day!

We were off Cape Race on Monday 27th January. The temperature was 10 degrees below zero, and our ropes and rails were covered in thick ice. On Friday, the last day of January, the weather deteriorated further when a gale sprang up. Our convoy was then joined by HMS King George V, which had been across to the United States with Lord Halifax, and joined us on our starboard side. Later in the day, we began taking on heavy seas.

(Editor's note: Lord Halifax was Foreign Secretary in P.M. Chamberlain's cabinet, continuing in P.M. Churchill's war cabinet, before being sent to the US as the UK Ambassador. He was charged with seeking aid from the (then neutral) US. The battleship, HMS King George V, would later the same year become Flagship of the Home Fleet and a major protagonist in the sinking of the German Battle Cruiser Bismarck, before going on to serve throughout the war in all three major naval theatres.)

On the 4th of February 1941, our position was 61.18N, 20W. HMS King George V and our escort ships had now left the convoy. Thursday morning saw the rough weather continuing, resulting in my cabin once again being flooded. In the late afternoon, the convoy was reformed into two lines astern. By the time I retired below at 9 p.m., we were within the protection of the Hebrides and heading south. We arrived at the Liverpool Bar on Saturday, where we dropped anchor for the night and docked on Sunday. Thereafter, whilst coming down the Irish Sea, my cabin, which I had finished cleaning, was swamped once again by a large wave.

(Author's note: Unfortunately, I have no record, nor any memory, of the following period until Sunday 23rd February, when we sailed out to sea again.)

It was Wednesday 26ᵗʰ February and our position was 55.5N, 14W. I was wakened about 1 a.m. by loud voices and heard an explosion. Going on deck, I was told there had been an earlier explosion before midnight. Almost immediately, there was another terrific 'bang' and the ship astern of us was setting off flares. There was another great flash as she listed heavily to port, after which red lights were hoisted on her mast. It was a clear night and the lights that were seen on the surface were presumed to be from lifeboats.

Fig.16 Author in Peder Bogen Radio Room

When daylight came, there were four ships missing from the convoy. I had washed and shaved and was lying on my settee at 10 a.m. when I heard yet another explosion, followed by gunfire. I rushed out to our port side and saw an enemy bomber quite low in the sky. Our escorts were putting up a barrage of shots in defence. One ship was on fire with fierce flames and escaping steam pouring from it. We then saw its lifeboats leaving the ship.

Whilst on watch at 6:15 p.m., I heard the sound of a ship's whistle and a destroyer's siren. On jumping up and looking through the aft-facing porthole I saw three low-flying bombers. They were approaching the convoy from astern and in line-abreast formation. Escorts and ships in the convoy engaged them immediately with rapid fire. Running out on deck, I saw the first plane to attack drop its bombs above a small ship. Fortunately, they missed their intended target. The second plane attacked the ship abreast of us on our port side, making a direct hit on her fo'c'sle.

The first plane, meanwhile, returned to make a second attack on another ship, but again it was unsuccessful, its bombs falling into the sea close to the stern of the ship. Meanwhile, the third plane, which at the outset looked as if it was coming over our column, veered off at the last minute to the column on our starboard side. It was successful in hitting one of the ships there, and dense clouds of steam began escaping, presumably from its engine room.

The stricken ship on our port side had begun to drift and the crew appeared to be having difficulty launching their lifeboats.

Fig.17 Stricken convoy vessel following aerial attack

One boat was dangling uselessly in an almost vertical position, and, after managing to launch a second, the ship seemed to drift down upon them. By this time, the steel plates at the bow section were opened outwards and appeared white-hot. The first bomber returned, flying again right up the column on our starboard side, with every ship firing as it passed. I distinctly saw two bombs drop as he flew over one ship, but thankfully, they fell harmlessly into the sea. Having gone up the column, the pilot swung wide of the convoy, returning to successfully attack a lagging ship failing to keep up with the rest of the convoy. A great deal of smoke was seen arising from this ship.

Whilst the action was on-going, I had been going from one side of the ship to the other and, whilst I had been on the port side, the ship on the other side – which had been hit in the engine room – had apparently reared up on its stern before sliding into the depths. Later that night, at 17 degrees west, the convoy broke up and we separated to continue on our individual routes. On Friday, 28th February, and in heavy seas, we passed close to the ship that had been Commodore of our convoy. We later learned that during the week ending 1st March, no less than twenty-nine ships had been lost to enemy action!

(Author's note: Regretfully, Diary notes after 28th February, and up until April 21st, 1941, are missing. On the latter date, our return voyage ended at Lough Foyle in Northern Ireland. However, with the aid of a pay-slip covering this period, I can see that I drew money whilst in the Dutch West Indies (probably Curaçao) on 17th and 22nd March, but nothing more until 23rd April when we were lying in Lough Foyle.)

Our Irish destination came as a great surprise as we were supposed to be heading for Liverpool. It was only when we approached the Northern Irish coast, we were ordered to break from the convoy and proceed into Lough Foyle. We anchored off the village of Moville in Eire to act as supply ship, transferring our cargo of oil to various vessels as required. When we wished to go ashore, we had to signal the shore for a small launch to come out. However, we only had the use of a rope ladder to get on and off the ship. The captain had refused to allow a gangway to be lowered, much to the disgust of the first R/O, who had quite a girth and was unable to negotiate a rope ladder. He was, therefore, never ashore during our three-week stay, but he was compensated, in part, by having the ferryman bring him bottles of the native brew.

The wives of the chief mate and chief engineer came across from Scotland and stayed in McKinney's, the local hotel. The third R/O and myself also stayed the night there on one or two occasions for bed and breakfast. The breakfasts were terrific, and I can still picture the hams hanging in the kitchen. The third R/O's parents also came across and visited the ship. His father was captain of the SS Athenia, the Donaldson Passenger Liner which had been sunk in the North Atlantic by a German torpedo less than eight hours after the declaration of war on 3rd September 1939. The ship had a complement of over one thousand, four hundred persons on-board including crew. Of the one hundred and twelve who lost their lives, sixty-nine were women and sixteen children.

Moville was a lovely spot and was the home of the famous General Montgomery. We were also able to visit Londonderry and most of the crew, including myself, were indeed sorry when we had to leave. During the last week,

I had made the acquaintance of a young lady from Derry who, as it happened, I hadn't seen or heard the last of. My undying memory of Lough Foyle is standing on deck in the spring evenings, looking across to Moville and the small cottages on the hillside behind. The picture was completed by the smell of peat smoke drifting down and over the lough. It was a magical sight.

A Greek ship, the SS Czikos, was lying nearby having arrived a few days prior to us. She had left Gibraltar with a cargo of steel destined for the UK but had been attacked by bombers in the Bay of Biscay, resulting in her bridge being shot away. Their third mate and the seaman at the wheel were killed, and two of the engine-room crew were wounded. The second engineer took over control of the engine-room crew, some of whom had deserted their posts, and the ship was eventually able to limp into the waters of Lough Foyle.

The engineer in question was a lady, Miss Victoria Drummond, and a godchild of Queen Victoria. She was awarded an MBE and a Lloyds Medal for her services at sea. The chief engineer, who was Yugoslavian, fell under suspicion because of his behaviour. He was duly arrested along with another four of the engine-room crew and taken to London under armed guard. During our stay, I saw Miss Drummond on at least one occasion when dining in the local hotel with her captain, who was believed to be Irish. They did not seem inclined to make conversation, perhaps understandably so, with Moville being over the border.

(Author's note: Miss Drummond's niece, Cherry Drummond, the 16th Baroness Strange of Megginch Castle, Errol, near Perth, was responsible for having a book published in 1994/5 spanning her famous aunt's life - "The Remarkable Life of Victoria Drummond, Marine Engineer". I was indebted to her for correcting me on some details of the episode I refer to.)

We sailed out of Lough Foyle in the early morning of Tuesday 13th May to join a westbound convoy. On the following day, we heard the amazing news of Hitler's Deputy, Rudolph Hess, and his ill-fated mission to negotiate peace, his solo flight from Germany across the North Sea, and subsequent landing in Lanarkshire, Scotland, leading to his arrest and lifetime incarceration.

Our journey was uneventful until the following Monday when we ran into fog which resulted in the convoy breaking up at 4 a.m. the next morning. Later the same day, we heard distress messages from four ships that had been torpedoed. One of those had been in our convoy and was only sixty miles away from our position. Whilst out on deck, I heard a tremendous explosion which must have been some distance away as there was nothing visible on the horizon. The following day, a US coast guard cutter approached us at close quarters and signalled that she was one of three vessels searching for survivors of the SS Marconi, which had also been part of our convoy.

On Friday 23rd May, I intercepted a message from the SS Felix which stated that she was *'still afloat'*. On the following day (Empire Day), we heard on the news of the sinking of the HMS Hood off the coast of Greenland by the German battleship Bismarck. There were only three survivors from the one thousand, four hundred and eighteen souls on-board. We had run into very thick fog at this time and it lasted for two whole days.

Only 4 days later, on Tuesday 27th May, we heard with some relief of the sinking of the Bismarck. This had included action by HMS King George V which had sailed alongside us in convoy on our previous crossing. Five days later, we arrived in New York Harbour. As it was my first visit, I was a bit overwhelmed by it all, but delighted to see the magnificent Statue of Liberty. I was lucky to have the opportunity to travel to the top of the Empire State Building and visit the famous Coney Island fun-fair.

We did not leave New York until Thursday 19th June, heading once again for Curaçao, where we arrived eight days later on Friday 27th. On our arrival, some leaflets were delivered to the ship advertising a 'Hockey Game' to be played two days later on the occasion, I believe, of the birthday of Prince Bernhard (of the Netherlands). One of the competing teams was the Queen's Own Cameron Highlanders and the other was a local 'Combined Outfit'. This was to be followed by the 'Sounding of the Retreat' by the Cameron Highlanders and the King's Own Shropshire Light Infantry. Proceeds from the event were for Prince Bernhard's Committee supporting aid for British Aircraft Production.

(Editor's Note: Prince Bernhard, after fleeing with Dutch troops to the UK, was in various forms of active service throughout the war, including an RAF Squadron. He achieved high military rank and attended armistice negotiations and the German surrender in the Netherlands. A German by birth, his early wish to work with British Intelligence was not granted but, through his friendship with King George VI, he was included in Military briefings. This had required, at the request of Churchill, the Prince being vetted by MI6 officer (and future 'James Bond' author) Ian Fleming - who, as it happens, receives a further mention later in this book. Considered a real war hero to the Dutch people, King George VI was quoted as saying of Prince Bernhard, "Of all the people I know, Prince Bernhard was the only one who enjoyed the war.")

Unfortunately, we were unable to witness any part of the advertised sporting event, as, having completed loading our cargo of oil, we once again sailed off, albeit this time in a different direction. Our destination was Sierra Leone in West Africa, and after an uneventful journey, we dropped anchor on July 18th in the large bay at Freetown. During our five-day stay, during which time we transferred our cargo to other ships requiring refuelling, shore leave was not allowed. However, as before, we were kept entertained by the locals in their canoes attempting to sell, amongst other things, fruit and eggs. Being open to the sea, and somewhat vulnerable to enemy attack, the bay was continually 'swept' by a low-flying seaplane.

We left Freetown and returned to Curaçao for reloading on August 6th when, to our surprise and initial disappointment, we learned we were to repeat the voyage to Freetown. Disappointment soon passed when we thought of the pleasures of sailing in the Tropics as opposed to the North Atlantic. This was enhanced by the fact we also had the makeshift canvas swimming pool back on deck.

Leaving Curaçao two days later, we proceeded to Freetown, arriving there on the 28th. We sailed again on the 2nd of September after our cargo had been unloaded. When we left Freetown on this occasion, I had to type out a new Crew List for the captain as we had two passengers on-board. They were husband and wife, who had been studying and collecting rare specimens of flowers and insect-life in the jungle for some considerable time. He was a South African, and she, a Canadian. On the amended crew-list, the lady was put down as 'Stewardess' and the gentleman as 'Supercargo'.

We soon learned the couple had actually left Freetown as passengers on another ship a week or two previously, but unfortunately, it had been torpedoed and sunk soon after leaving port. The tragedy of it all was compounded by the fact, not only had they lost all their personal belongings – leaving them only the tropical clothes they had been wearing at the time – but they had lost several crates of specimens. These had been collected over a very long and arduous time and under difficult and dangerous conditions. We felt so sorry for them and it was obvious how shattered they were by the experience. They kept very much to themselves during the four weeks they were with us.

We docked at Aruba on Friday 19th September and loading began immediately. The following day, we left for Halifax, NS. However, we were later diverted to Sydney, Cape Breton, where we docked on the 30th. It was here that our two passengers disembarked to a much lower temperature – yet still wearing their tropical clothing. However, they were now, at last, in a safe haven.

We left Sydney on Monday 6th October to join the east-bound convoy (SC-48) from Halifax. The journey was uneventful until the early hours of Wednesday 15th when I was awakened by the sound of two explosions. They were not exceptionally loud, but nevertheless, I rose to go on deck. It was dark and there was nothing to be seen, so I returned to my bunk. When morning broke, it was revealed that two ships were now missing from the convoy. Between the hours of 9 and 10 p.m., the escort ships kept on dropping depth charges in an effort to keep the ever-present U-boats at bay.

By the time full daylight came, yet another ship was missing and, later in the afternoon, more escorts arrived. These included the American destroyer, USS Kearny, which had been escorting another east-bound convoy, but had been ordered back to our defence. This proved to be just in time! Throughout the night, from 9 p.m. until the early hours, we experienced more than five hours of sheer bedlam. The scene was rent with explosions, depth charges being fired off, flames rising from a number of burning ships, screaming sirens and ships' whistles seemingly going on non-stop. This turned out to be my worst sustained experience in six years of service at sea!

When daylight came, we discovered that no less than seven vessels were missing, including the USS Kearny. We observed a rescue ship looking for survivors whilst planes were patrolling overhead. We later heard, however, that the Kearny, with a jagged hole in her starboard side, had managed to limp into an Icelandic port. A member of the crew related his story of the events in a newspaper as follows:

"We joined the convoy in the late afternoon as it was re-forming after the first attack. The second one began after dark and everything was soon lit up by flames from three oil tankers. A pack of submarines lay awash, firing torpedoes into the slow-moving ships. At 1.30 a.m., a U-boat surfaced between the Kearny and the convoy, and fired three times, hitting us amidships. The explosion knocked back the forward funnel, snapping the cord of the siren which screamed incessantly."

"Pack of U-Boats" in Kearny Attack

HOW the United States destroyer Kearney dropped depth-charges in the vicinity of a "pack of U-boats" was described in messages published in the American press yesterday.

The story of what happened was told by a member of the crew of the Kearny. The destroyer was torpedoed on October 17 near Iceland, but reached port under its own power.

"We had been escorting a west-bound convoy," he said, "but we were ordered to swing back to join an east-bound convoy—protected by Canadian corvettes—which had been attacked.

"We joined the convoy late in the afternoon, just as it was resuming after the first attack by the submarines. We also hunted for survivors.

The second attack began after dark, but everything was soon lit up by the flames from three tankers. A pack of submarines lay awash firing torpedoes into the slow-moving ships.

"The Kearny dropped several depth charges in order to scare hell out of the submarines.

"At 1.30 a.m on October 17 a U-boat surfaced between the Kearny and the convoy with its engines cut off," the man continued. "She must have been very close. She fired three times, hitting the Kearny amidships The explosion knocked back the forward funnel and snapped the cord of the siren. which screamed incessantly."

The Kearny, with a jagged hole in her starboard side limped into port escorted by the Greer—which itself has been attacked by a Nazi submarine.

Fig.18 'Kearny Incident' report

(Editor's note: In what became known as 'The Kearny Incident', the action was notable as the US had not yet formally entered the war. Records state that the Kearny, having been engaged in convoy ON-24, was called upon to assist the British convoy SC-48 when it and its Canadian escorts had become overwhelmed by a Wolf Pack of German U-boats. After dropping depth charges and continuing the barrage overnight, the Kearny was subsequently struck on its starboard side by a torpedo fired from U-568, losing eleven men with twenty-two

injured. The incident was specifically cited as a provocation in Adolf Hitler's declaration of war against the US. The Kearny survived to serve on the North Atlantic convoys as well as a number of other naval theatres including the Mediterranean and the Pacific.)

It was Sunday 19th October and we were into a gale with very heavy seas, which led to all vessels having to 'heave-to'. On coming off watch at 8 p.m., I got drenched to the skin on the way to my cabin. There was a great improvement in the weather the next morning at 4 a.m. when I took up watch. Only one or two scattered ships could be seen and we proceeded alone with no escort.

We eventually entered the River Clyde on Tuesday 21st October and proceeded to Loch Long where we anchored. One week later, I left the Peder Bogen, for what turned out to be the last time. A customs officer took two rolls of film from me for censoring. One contained some shots taken during the submarine attack.

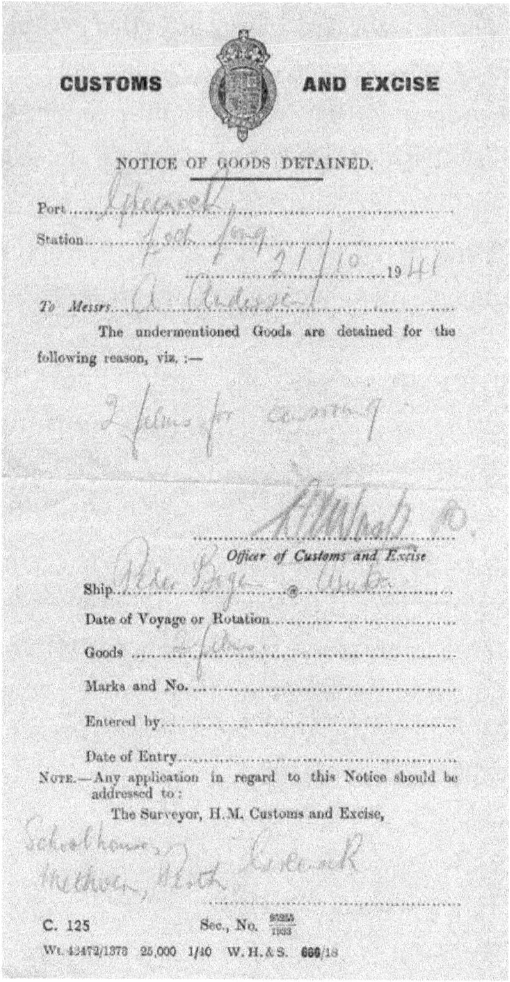

CUSTOMS AND EXCISE

NOTICE OF GOODS DETAINED.

Port..

Station..

21/10 1941

To Messrs..

The undermentioned Goods are detained for the following reason, viz. :—

2 films for censoring

....
Officer of Customs and Excise

Ship..

Date of Voyage or Rotation..

Goods..

Marks and No..

Entered by..

Date of Entry..

Note.—Any application in regard to this Notice should be addressed to:

The Surveyor, H.M. Customs and Excise,

....

C. 125 Sec., No. $\frac{86255}{1933}$

Wt. 42472/1373 25,000 1/40 W. H. & S. 666/18

Fig.19 Customs receipt for photo film censorship

Before leaving Peder Bogen, I had indicated to the captain that I did not wish to remain with the ship. This was because of the deteriorating relationship between the first R/O and myself, which he understood.

Chapter 5 - SS Sourabaya

Fig.20 SS Sourabaya

I had been at home for about ten or eleven days when Salvesen contacted me on 19th November. They asked if I was available to join the SS Sourabaya, which was lying in Glasgow. Having to make a quick decision, I travelled through to Glasgow, signed on and joined the ship with my gear the following day.

We sailed from the Clyde later in the week and had an uneventful passage to Halifax, where we dropped off several passengers, before continuing to New York. Whilst we were loading there, the December 7th Japanese attack on Pearl Harbour took place and shattered any feelings of neutrality in some sections of the American population.

When we left New York, besides our main cargo of oil, we also had additional deck cargo. This included two large motor launches and large drums of aniline (used in the production of chemicals and dyes). We also had a fellow R/O on-board as a DBS passenger, returning home after having spent six months in a US hospital.

Our trip home was without incident. We spent Christmas 1941 at sea and arrived in the Clyde on December 29th. This resulted in my getting home for Hogmanay, New Year's Day and, of course, my birthday the following day. I received a surprise call on New Year's Day from Stella, the young lady I had met in Ireland.

Around midnight on 12th January 1942, we left the Clyde, once more heading for New York via Halifax. After a week or so, bad weather set in. This eventually resulted in the convoy breaking up, with ships going their separate ways. After calling at Halifax, we continued on to New York. Because enemy submarines had commenced an intensive campaign along the US Atlantic coast, we were now sailing much closer to land. A day or two before reaching our destination, we ran aground on a sandbank. Fortunately, we managed to get off again after two hours or so. Thereafter, we continued without incident into New York Harbour.

Soon after dropping anchor on 28th January, we were visited by US Coast Guard officers. After interviewing every member of the crew, they issued us identification cards with a unique 'Alien Registration Number'. The cards also bore a passport-type photograph and fingerprint of the recipient. This was a new requirement because of America now being at war.

Before loading commenced, we had to go into dry-dock for investigation and check-up to see if the hull had suffered any damage as a result of us running aground, but thankfully, we got the all-clear.

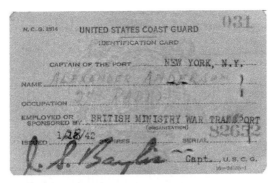

Fig.21 US Alien Registration Photo ID card

During our stay, we were able to see several well-known performers on the theatre stage, including the Mills Brothers, Martha Raye and the comedy trio The Three Stooges. One night, three of us got talking to two Englishmen in a restaurant bar. They turned out to be brothers Arthur and Emlyn from Surrey. They were touring the country presenting on stage a novelty Hand-Balancing Act billed as the Equillo Brothers.

They told us they were to be performing at the famous Waldorf Astoria Hotel on January 31st, the occasion being the Annual Banquet of the National League of Wholesale Fresh Fruit and Vegetable Distributors. Asking if we were interested, they offered to meet us outside the hotel and show us up to the balcony. From there, we could look down on the whole proceedings, which were taking place in the Grand Ballroom below.

The third R/O, George Plante, and myself decided that we could not refuse the brothers' invitation. However, this was the chance to get into the Waldorf, even though we would be looking down enviously at the 62 tables with 542 guests tucking into a lavish dinner. We could only read the menu which was shown in a booklet of the event which we received as a souvenir. Still, it was a night to remember and our hosts, who were one of five acts on stage, gave a fantastic performance which was enthusiastically applauded by the audience.

After taking on our cargo of oil, we moved to one of the Cunard Line piers to take on deck cargo. We found ourselves on the next pier to the large French liner SS Normandie, which had suffered damage from a fire onboard two or three days before. Our deck cargo was quite a surprise - eighteen fighter planes and one bomber, all minus their wings, of course.

We re-crossed the Atlantic without incident, reaching Liverpool once again on March 13th. I was able to travel home for a brief two-day visit, before we set off once again, seven days later. When we arrived at Halifax, again without incident, we received some alarming news.

My previous ship, the Peder Bogen, had been sunk seven hundred miles from Curaçao. It had loaded its oil cargo, and was, I believe, *en-route* to Freetown, Sierra Leone. My thoughts, of course, were with those friends on-board. We had served together for eighteen months through some dark days and nights and had parted only six months earlier. Before leaving Halifax, the local agent told the captain some hopeful news. There was an unconfirmed report of one boat-load of survivors being picked-up and they were *en-route* to New York.

With enemy U-boats still very active on the American coast, we were directed on 13th April to proceed even closer to the coast. This resulted in us going through the Cape Cod Canal. Keeping to the inside of Long Island, we proceeded down the East River, under several bridges, including the Brooklyn Bridge, and finally, into the safety of New York harbour, where we docked. It was quite an experience sailing under the bridges. We were lying very high in the water because of the shallow waters we had been sailing in. This made it more likely that the top of our foremast would be in danger of fouling on the underside of the bridges. This required the ship to sail strictly to the part allowing the highest elevation. As we approached one structure, our Norwegian captain said to the pilot,

"I will give you a bottle of whisky if you only take off the tip of the mast".

However, the pilot knew his job and we made it damage-free.

When our agent's representative came on-board, we were relieved to hear survivors from one of the Peder Bogen lifeboats had indeed arrived in New York. On learning the name of the hotel where the survivors were staying, two or three of us immediately got on the underground and made our way to visit them. They comprised the occupants in the lifeboat headed by the chief mate, including my 'friend' Snowy, the first R/O. I did not think it appropriate at the time to dare ask how he managed to get into the lifeboat, considering he had been unable to negotiate the rope ladder on a previous occasion!

The survivors told us how the ship was suddenly hit by torpedoes. This was followed by the attacking submarine surfacing, and firing on the stricken vessel which, by now, was on fire. They rowed away from the scene as quickly as possible fearing a large explosion, as their cargo was oil. In all the confusion and failing light, they became separated from the other lifeboat. It was quite some time later before the flames suddenly disappeared, signifying the Peder Bogen had gone to its watery grave. There was still no report at this time of the captain's lifeboat.

However, on returning by underground train to the ship, I was glancing through the pages of a newspaper which I had purchased earlier at a kiosk. Suddenly, at the bottom of a page, my eyes were caught by the headline of a single-column, two-inch press release:

'*21 SURVIVORS LAND AT LISBON*'.

"Lisbon, April 12 (AP). The Spanish tanker Gobeo landed 21 survivors from the Norwegian tanker Pederbogen, reported sunk March 23 in the Caribbean by two torpedoes from a German submarine. The crew of 53 took to lifeboats, and 21 survivors, including Captain W. Dawson, in one lifeboat, were picked up by the Gobeo four days after the sinking." (Lloyds does not list a Norwegian tanker Pederbogen, but it does list a British tanker of 9,741 tons of that name)."

The following year, a follow-up article to this story appeared in the Scottish press. The captain, with several of his officers and men, had made a heroic bid to save the vessel. Awards for bravery and skill in the face of great danger and difficulty had been announced:

"Captain William Thomson Dawson (33) with two of his officers and fireman – all Scots – who, with others of their shipmates, have been decorated for their bravery and skill in saving lives and trying to save their torpedoed ship in most dangerous circumstances. Captain Dawson, Edinburgh, "showed splendid courage, resource and leadership throughout," according to the official citation. "He has been awarded the O.B.E. ... The M.B.E. goes to Third Engineer Stephen J.M. Tyson (41) ... Fourth Engineer David G. Mackenzie (26) ... and Sixth Engineer Glencoe Macdonald ... William C. Murdoch (27), Fireman ... and William Sandilands (40) ... receive the B.E.M."

Fig.22 SS Peder Bogen survivor bravery awards

We sailed from New York again around the 19th of April. In addition to our cargo of oil, we had additional deck cargo comprising tanks and planes. We also had some passengers, including DBS from lost ships, and of course, Snowy from Peder Bogen, who was most keen to travel home with us. Thankfully, the voyage home was uneventful and we arrived back in the Clyde on May 15th. I managed to get home for two days, before rejoining the ship in the Gare Loch. The famous liner RMS Queen Mary was also lying there at this time.

We left from the Clyde again on 19th May. I was delighted to find we had an old friend of mine on-board as a passenger. This was chief engineer D.C. Waddell, formerly of the Peder Bogen. I envied him when I heard he was *en-route* to Vancouver, to bring a ship back home. It was an uneventful passage and, as before, we didn't call at Halifax. We had to take the coastal journey through the Cape Cod Canal and the East River to New York. Once again, this was due to the continuing U-boat activity on the American coast.

We arrived in New York on 7th June, the same day the Battle of Midway was won in the Pacific, and exactly six months after one of my previous visits that coincided with the attack on Pearl Harbour. We left New York two days later, and without having some repairs done that we had expected. This was a disappointment as it meant we had only one day's shore leave before we sailed in convoy again. We were close inshore to Delaware Bay, in single-line ahead, and through the narrow Delaware to Chesapeake Bay Canal. As we were a larger ship, we were at times quite close to the banks on either side and often hitting the bottom, which churned up the muddy waters. It was quite an experience, made worse by the mosquitoes which were diabolical during this journey.

We lay at Hampton Roads in the bay for two to three days. The delay was due to two ships having been sunk by mines immediately outside the bay. When we sailed south again, it was a slow-moving convoy, which was never a good thing. As if to labour the point, one of the ships was then sunk by another mine. Thereafter, the escort vessels dropped many depth charges, whilst planes kept patrolling overhead.

One morning, we intercepted a message from one of the planes stating it was trailing a damaged submarine slightly ahead of us. Later the same afternoon, a tanker in the outside starboard column sighted the U-boat and bravely attempted to ram it. We never did hear the outcome, but the escorts continued to drop many depth charges in the area as a result.

On reaching Key West, Florida on 25th June, the convoy broke up and we went our separate ways. We headed into the Gulf of Mexico making for our destination of Texas City, where we arrived four days later. We got some surprise once ashore, as it was no city as we knew it, being more like a village to us. In fact, it only existed as a storage and distribution port for the oilfields of Texas. However, it proved to be another new experience, as one thing we did manage to get was genuine Southern-Fried Chicken 'n chips. A nice change for us all.

With our cargo loaded, we left Texas City. Arriving at the mouth of the Mississippi River around 6:30 p.m. on Thursday, we proceeded upstream to the City of New

Orleans. We dropped anchor on Friday 3rd July around breakfast time, and one of the first ships we saw lying there was another Salvesen factory ship, the SS Southern Empress. New Orleans was completely different to Texas City, and we thoroughly enjoyed our stay there.

One remarkable sight was the activity in the shipyards on the riverside. With so many merchant ships being lost by enemy action, America came up with the idea of undertaking the mass production of ships. Instead of riveting the steel plates together, they welded them which was so much quicker. Another novelty was, instead of launching the ships astern first, they launched them side-on into the river. This was necessary because of the river's lack of width. Known as 'Liberty Ships', they were a godsend for the allied merchant fleets at a time when losses were very high. Although, it must be said, because of the nature of their construction, not all losses were caused by enemy action.

Invasion Barges were also being constructed in New Orleans. This was the reason for our visit, and we took on a quantity of these as deck cargo before sailing in the evening. At 2 a.m. the next morning, it was necessary to stop the engine for a short period to undertake some repairs. However, when we attempted to move again it was discovered the ship had dragged anchor, and we ran aground. It was midday before a tug arrived to pull us free. Orders were then received telling us to return up-river so divers could inspect the hull and rudder for any signs of damage. Getting the all-clear, we set off again on the evening of 14th July and, reaching the delta by about 6:30 p.m. the next day, we anchored until daylight.

Whilst close to St. Joseph Point the following evening, a steam pipe burst in the engine room, and we had to stop and drop anchor. Repairs could not be undertaken on-board, which resulted in the chief engineer being rowed ashore at 6:30 a.m. the following morning. He took a section of damaged pipe with him in an effort to have it repaired by brazing. Thankfully, the chief arrived back with the repaired pipe some four or five hours later. However, it was not without some welcome help and good fortune. He had landed at a fairly isolated spot and there was no one with facilities for carrying out the repair, but luckily, someone had mentioned there was a paper mill some miles away he could try. So, with the assistance of a friendly truck owner, this is what he did, and the mill-workers gladly obliged by carrying out the repair.

Thus, we were able to set off again shortly after noon. Later in the day, a message was received stating that a submarine had been sighted in the approaches to the Mississippi. On Saturday night, we moved closer inshore about 10 p.m. and dropped anchor until 2 a.m. This was so we could reach Key West in daylight at around 9 a.m. We then had to wait some time for a pilot to take us to a safe anchorage, and we finally dropped anchor at about 4:30 p.m.

Monday was a glorious day with not a cloud in the sky, a calm sea and practically no wind. I was talking to the third mate on deck when the steward approached us and said,

"What about going out on a lifeboat for a nice sail?"

Actually, neither of us was too keen, wishing to undergo as little exertion as possible. However, the steward persisted and said if the sail was put up, there would be little for us to do. We could then lie back in the sun and enjoy the light breeze off the water. Struggling for another reason, he added that it would be an opportunity to make sure the lifeboat was indeed seaworthy, in the event we might have the misfortune to need it later.

Thus, against our better judgement, and with the steward's cheery words ringing in our ears, we lowered the boat. After rowing a short distance from the ship, we raised the sail to catch the very slight breeze. Initially, it was indeed fantastic lying back in the warmth of the sun, listening to the lapping of the water. We were also looking with interest at the varied collection of anchored ships as we sailed past. Time meant nothing, nor distance, until we suddenly realised the Sourabaya was now quite difficult to locate in the far distance.

Turning about, we retraced our course, but it soon became clear that we were making little progress. The lessening breeze was, at times, hardly filling the sail. The steward eventually said,

"You two take the oars for a spell and I'll steer meantime and relieve you later."

I have to say the steward was a big lad, carrying a lot of weight and not exactly a figure of athletic fitness. As time passed, our progress remained slow. The mate and I were beginning to feel the effects of our exertions under the relentless rays of the sun.

So, it was suggested by us that the self-appointed steersman might wish to carry out his earlier promise. However, our efforts were to no avail.

"You are doing fine!" he said. "There's no way I'm taking an oar – someone will come out and tow us back."

With evening coming on, and realising the steward appeared to be suffering more from exposure to the sun, we decided to press on. We eventually reached the ship in time for dinner but, unfortunately for my part, I was unable to sit down and partake of it. It was a day's outing to try and forget.

We sailed from Key West in convoy in the early hours of Wednesday 22nd July after experiencing a terrific thunderstorm during the night. Because of intense enemy activity on the American coast, we followed a route much further out to sea. We then continued direct towards Massachusetts Bay, where we dropped anchor on the evening of 26th July. On the following day, an OS (Ordinary Seaman) from our ship decided to go for a swim on his own, and found himself being carried away by a strong tide. Fortunately, his predicament was observed by a member of the crew of a Dutch ship lying astern of us. He promptly dived into the sea and rescued the lad. Unfortunately, this lesson was not learned by our messboy who, the very next day, repeated the exercise.

Only the presence of mind shown by one of our firemen saved the boy's life when he dived in after him. Upon reaching the boy, he managed to grab him, and as they were being carried past a US Army ship, the Fireman managed to grab hold of a ladder on the side of the vessel. Members of the US crew hauled them on-board and delivered them back to us later in one of their motor launches.

On the following day, we sailed back to New York, once again through the Cape Cod Canal, and via the East River. On the way down, I received a sea-bag made from strong canvas. It was made by an older member of the crew who was Norwegian and only known by the name Callopy. He had joined the ship in Norway before the country was invaded, and so was unable to return home. He was a very nice man and was listed on the ship's crew-list, rather historically, as Sailmaker. We anchored off Staten Island at about 10 p.m. and moved into dock the following evening. Testing of the emergency black-out arrangements and the warning sirens was being carried out today. On Sunday, we saw the liner, Queen Mary, pass down the river.

We left New York in the afternoon of Friday 7th August, having taken more deck cargo of Army Jeeps. In addition, we took passengers, including some 'Lascar' Seamen from India. They brought on board with them seven live sheep, allowing them to do their own ritual killing of fresh meat.

On Saturday forenoon, we anchored at Cape Cod and left the following afternoon for Boston, to await further additions to our convoy. Our departure from there on Thursday was delayed for several hours because of thick fog, and this persisted all the way to Halifax. We arrived there at midnight on the following day.

When daylight came, we could see two ships which had been victims of enemy submarines. One had its stern blown off by two torpedoes and the other (a tanker) had its forepart missing. We were able to get ashore for a brief visit to stretch our legs, but there was not too much to see anyway. However, we were surprised to meet a man who had travelled as a passenger with us on a previous trip.

On Sunday 16th August, we were again in convoy, the fog still persisting. On Tuesday, the fog cleared for a few hours in the morning and we were re-joined by two or three ships that had strayed during the night. However, we were still two vessels short of our original complement of thirty-three. The fog cleared away on Wednesday and the convoy was re-joined by a total of eleven ships which had gone missing. But still, there were some unaccounted for. The improved weather conditions continued as we sailed towards home unhindered. The only exception was when the course of the convoy was suddenly changed to a southerly direction. We learned this was caused by some unknown incident occurring towards the north of our position at that time.

On Thursday 27th August, we were appointed Commodore of the Clyde-bound ships, when we broke off from the main convoy during the evening. No sooner had we dropped anchor in Loch Long in western Scotland the following morning than we had dockers on-board removing the first of our deck cargo. This comprised nineteen barges and forty jeeps. As soon as the company representative arrived on-board, I learned that my third R/O, George Plante, and myself would receive shore leave until 26th September. We then moved up the Clyde to Bowling on Saturday 29th where our cargo of oil was to be discharged. I then said my farewells before heading home on Monday 31st August. Little did we know at that time how providential this would be in light of subsequent events!

Fig.23 Author writing home aboard SS Sourabaya

Following my period of shore leave, Salvesen's had no ships available, so I was automatically transferred to the Merchant Navy Shipping Pool. However, when a ship became available, I was taken back onto Salvesen's books again as from the 8th of October. I heard nothing more until the morning of 11th November, when a letter arrived from Salvesen's Marine Superintendent, Mr R.J. Leask. Expecting it would be announcing the offer of a ship, I hurriedly tore open the envelope and the letter's opening words stunned me rigid.

'We regret that owing to the fact that we have lost both the Empress and the Sourabaya ...' it continued, *'... we will have to transfer you to the pool'.* The devastating letter concluded, *'... No doubt you will have heard that Mr Ryrie lost his life.'*

He was the only R/O to be lost on the two ships. I was having breakfast with my parents when the letter came. I sat speechless, and it was some considerable time before I could read out loud to my parents the words relating to my last ship,

'The Sourabaya's lost!'

I had to hand the letter over to my parents to continue reading. I was simply unable to and felt completely shattered by the devastating news.

The following morning, I received a letter from George Plante, the third R/O who had left the fated Sourabaya along with me on 31st September. He had met one of the survivors in Edinburgh who had given him the details of the sinking. It was a very graphic and upsetting story!

The Sourabaya was homeward bound in mid-Atlantic when it was struck on the port bow by a torpedo, and immediately listed to port. As on previous voyages, she was carrying some DBS passengers who, given their recent experience, had panicked and run amok. When the alarm was rung for lifeboat stations, it was alleged there was utter confusion, leading to a situation where it was 'every man for himself'. Some lifeboats were launched but they were on the weather side, and so became dashed against the side of the ship. The survivor telling the story had been in a lifeboat for three and a half hours, before being rescued by a naval corvette. Unfortunately, during the rescue, an engineer was killed by being crushed between the lifeboat and the corvette.

The total loss of crew was said to be ninety-five. Included were the first, second and third mates as well as poor old Callopy, who had made the canvas sea bag for me on my last trip on Sourabaya. They were all incredibly good friends whom I shall never forget.

One fortunate man who escaped the tragedy was First R/O Mr Sprott, with whom I had first served on the New Sevilla, then, more recently, on the Sourabaya itself. It appeared he had missed the sailing time in New York, and so was not on-board for the fateful voyage. Like myself and George, he was also a fortunate man.

The Southern Empress, a sister ship, had been in another convoy and was hit by one torpedo. She endeavoured to make land, but unfortunately, some fourteen hours later, was struck by a further two torpedoes and sank. The survivors spent nine hours in lifeboats before being rescued.

(Editor Note: By way of a postscript, the name of George Plante, the often-mentioned 3rd R/O came to light, quite by chance, during editing research in 2023. Not only did it transpire that Plante was a survivor of the torpedoed Southern Empress (his next ship after Sourabaya) but his fascinating later life story was deemed worthy of some mention here.

On researching the Sourabaya convoy that left New York on 19th April 1942, a link to the Imperial War Museum London, revealed 1942-dated paintings of Sourabaya. Some of these paintings depicted deck cargo of planes and tanks, exactly as described by the author for that particular convoy. The artist was named as none other than, 'George Plante'.

Although not mentioned by the author in his original manuscript, it transpired that Plante studied art (in UK & pre-war Berlin) and, before joining-up, worked as a graphic artist. Continuing to paint at sea, his work became known in the US for its propaganda value. Not only was he commissioned to continue that work whilst at sea, but he came to the attention of a certain Naval Intelligence (MI6) officer, Ian Fleming, (who received an earlier mention in this book). Plante was later diverted to full-time covert work producing anti-Nazi propaganda material from his new posting in Cairo. Surviving the war, Plante continued in his chosen profession as an artist.

Plante's own story, 'Painting War: George Plante's Combat Art in World War II' (by Kathleen Broome Williams) only came into print in 2019. Williams, a Naval historian and Plante's own step-daughter, corroborates from Plante's prolific letter-writing, many of the incidents recounted by the author in this book. Despite leaving the ill-fated Sourabaya together on the same day, and Plante's correspondence on its demise, the author is not mentioned by name in Plante's memoir. It is with some regret that the author's letter from Plante did not survive the last 80 years.

Chapter 6 - SS Saluta

Fig.24 SS Saluta

I received a telephone call at home on 18th November 1942 from Salvesen saying they could offer me the position of second R/O on the SS Saluta, this being the only position available, due to the recent loss of ships. At the time of my leaving the Sourabaya, I was told my next position would be as first R/O, however, given the loss of ships, I had no hesitation in accepting the post.

I joined the ship two days later at South Shields. I found her to be in dry-dock undergoing a refit, which was to take some time. As a result, I used the time to attend a two-day Merchant Navy Anti-Aircraft (MN A/A) Gunnery

Course. I had to qualify in the firing, cleaning and oiling of the Oerlikon, Marlin and Hotchkiss machine-guns which were fitted on-board the ship.

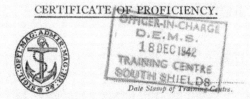

MERCHANT NAVY A/A GUNNERY COURSE.

CERTIFICATE OF PROFICIENCY.

OFFICER-IN-CHARGE
D.E.M.S.
18 DEC 1942
TRAINING CENTRE
SOUTH SHIELDS

Date Stamp of Training Centre.

Name A. ANDERSON

Rank or Rating Radio Officer - "SALUTA"

B. of T. or D.B. No.

has completed the Merchant Navy A/A Gunnery Course and is qualified in the firing and cleaning and oiling of * Oerlikon,Marlin,Hotchkiss.

2 day course.

Rank Lieutenant Commander.R.N.

D.E.M.S.
Training Centre SOUTH SHIELDS

* Insert types of guns and/or A/A devices.

(792) Wt. 11184/P5697 30m 5/42 S.E.R. Ltd. Gp. 671. [OVER

Fig.25 MN A/A Gunnery Course Certificate

It was mid-January 1943 before we were ready to depart the River Tyne at South Shields. We had some passengers on-board, one of whom joined us under rather mysterious circumstances, and whilst we were already underway. It was evening when we left the Tyne and rendezvoused with a launch with us to return the pilot to port. As he boarded the launch, several men came off and onto our vessel. They were there to deliver our 'passenger', who was in their 'close custody'. He was formally handed over, as a deportee, to the captain.

Our passenger turned out to be quite a character. It transpired he had US gangland associations. In the UK, he had been moving around within contrasting levels of society from barmaids to landed gentry. He gave the first R/O a bundle of letters with the request they be posted in the UK on our return. He also provided a New York telephone number of an apparently well-known gangster requesting to be told once the deportee was *'back in town'*!

We arrived in Methil Dock in the Firth of Forth a day later. We sailed again the day after as Commodore ship, leading a convoy bound for Loch Ewe in the northwest of Scotland. We dropped anchor in Loch Ewe on Tuesday in beautiful weather. As we were on our way out again on Friday, a message was received telling us to remain in the loch until the following Saturday.

On Sunday 24th January, we met up with the main convoy of approximately fifty-five ships coming up from the south. There was a heavy swell on the sea, and the weather continued to deteriorate. By Saturday, it was becoming steadily colder as we had sight of the coast of Greenland, and saw a patrolling seaplane overhead. On the following day, I had quite an argument with one of the mates (nicknamed 'Wu'). He thought, erroneously, that radio officers should take flag duties on the bridge in addition to their own regular shifts in the radio room.

On Monday, the first day of February, the sea was not quite so rough but we had heavy snow squalls. This continued into day three when we were moving in large areas of pack ice in a heavy swell. The temperature was seven degrees below zero. By the end of the week, it had become slightly warmer but misty. Some ships had left the convoy, heading for the Canadian Ports. When Sunday dawned, we could only see four other ships around us. By midday, the mist had cleared away and the missing vessels gradually returned, and the convoy re-formed once again. Later the same night, we encountered rough seas which continued with a very heavy, head-on swell and, as a result, we were making very little head-way. Unsurprisingly, I felt a cold coming on and so took to my bunk fortified by a tot of rum and two aspirin.

At 4.30 a.m., I was wakened by a loud crash followed by a violent shaking of the ship. I got out of my bunk in record time. Pulling on my trousers, I suddenly realised it had all gone ominously quiet. As it transpired, my rude awakening had been caused by a big sea crashing onto the ship. During the day, strong winds persisted, but the sea was not quite so rough. It turned out fine in the evening as the convoy formed into a single column. We arrived in New York on Wednesday 10th February and anchored in the harbour. Two days later, we shifted to Bayonne, New Jersey. Whilst there, the temperature fell to eight degrees below zero, and we also suffered a steering-gear cylinder burst. This led to us being towed to the Hudson Pier in New York for repairs.

On Tuesday, March 23rd, we finally left the Pier and dropped anchor off the Statue of Liberty in the harbour. On the following day, I accompanied the captain to the usual pre-sailing briefing conference on-shore. In the early hours of Thursday, whilst still at anchor, we were hit by another vessel which had dragged anchor. Fortunately, no real damage was done and we were able to sail as planned later in the day in good weather. Once again, we had taken on our usual cargo of oil, plus a few DBS passengers. The good weather continued until Saturday night when we encountered fog, which was followed on Sunday by some colder and rougher conditions.

When Monday dawned, it was very cold with the ship completely iced over, and the convoy in disarray. I was quite shocked to learn there had been a tragic fatal accident during the night. One of the DBS passengers had been found lying dead on deck in the early hours. Why he was there, no one knew, but with the prevailing conditions, it would not have been wise for him to be there on his own. At 4 p.m., the captain ordered the ship's engine to be stopped and he conducted a brief burial service. The body, wrapped in a canvas shroud, was gently and solemnly committed to the deep waters.

Despite being a daily target when at sea, and having witnessed losses on a number of convoys, this was the only burial at sea on a ship I was actually serving on. It was a very moving experience, and one I would never forget.

By the time the engine was re-started, the rest of the convoy was quite some distance ahead, and we eventually realised we would be unable to make up the resultant gap. The captain had a difficult decision to make - either to struggle on alone and completely unprotected, or to make for Halifax. Although Halifax was only two days away, it had to be considered due to the knowledge of a message we had received of an enemy submarine being detected only 35 miles outside of the port. To Halifax was the decision, and no one disagreed. That night continued to be cold and bleak. When Tuesday dawned, things improved steadily and there was quiet relief all round when we dropped anchor in the harbour at Halifax on Wednesday 31st March.

On Monday, we went alongside in order to take on some more cargo and passengers. Three days later, we were still there. A few of us had been ashore for a walk around and, when returning to the wharf, the third R/O suddenly let out a shout,

"Look at that!"

This turned out to be the Canadian Navy Frigate K103, which was tied up alongside. The Third became quite ecstatic, and cried out,

"I cannot believe it," he continued before explaining,

"… that's the Frigate that rescued me when my last ship was torpedoed!"

Two officers who were involved in his rescue were still serving on-board K-103, and so we were all invited to attend a great reunion between the rescued and his rescuers. The Third related how he had enjoyed the food served on the K-103. He expressed an especially fond memory of the lashings of genuine maple syrup which seemed to be poured over everything. This resulted in his receiving a jar of the natural product when we finally left the Frigate.

The third R/O was a well-built chap, and I can vouch for his enjoyment of food. When we ate ashore in New York, he inevitably ordered a fried onion omelette and chips, at the same time telling the waiter or waitress he wanted extra onions on the side. When the dish arrived, it was quickly given the once-over and, if not satisfied with the quantity of onions, the bearer was requested to take it back to the kitchen for replenishment.

The new convoy left Halifax on April 15th in improving weather conditions. On Saturday, it was a beautiful sunny day and the sea was like a mirror. Unfortunately, the escorts had to keep dropping depth charges around the convoy as, once again, intruders were around. During the night, it was thought we might have to transfer one of the passengers to the hospital ship in the convoy. However, later in the morning, his condition improved, so this was no longer necessary. On Tuesday, the convoy made a sudden drastic alteration of course, making us alert to the fact the enemy were still in our vicinity. The weather remained good but colder, and we now had some snow showers at night.

There was a rude interruption at 6 a.m. when depth charges were again being dropped. Later in the morning, one of the ships reported a U-boat had been seen within the convoy. More depth charges followed. Later in the day, we found ourselves in thick ice with some icebergs around. After trying to find our way through, an urgent message came from the Commodore to all ships in the convoy:

'You are standing into danger, act independently.'

Thus, we all had to do a turn-about. By Thursday, the convoy had again re-formed which was fortunate as once again, during the day, we had another abrupt change of course, U-boats having been reported ahead of us. This threat persisted when a message was received on Friday 23rd April, advising us of U-boat sightings some 210 miles ahead of our position. We had more snow squalls during the day and, at one point, sighted a fairly large iceberg. Depth charges were again dropped during the evening. By Sunday, the weather was much warmer and we had another course alteration.

On Tuesday, our escorts were augmented by the arrival of a further two destroyers. On the following day, weather conditions worsened again just as U-boats were reported in our vicinity. Iceland-bound ships now broke off from the convoy.

The weather had improved by Sunday but it was dull and misty. I told the captain today I would like to sign-off when we reached port if this were possible. However, I hastened to add that I would be pleased to re-join again at the end of their next trip if he so wished.

We arrived at the Mersey River Bar during the night of Monday 3rd May. Moving up the river to Liverpool the next morning, we dropped anchor. The passengers were taken off by launch, and I followed them three days later for a much-anticipated respite from the North Atlantic.

As previously hoped, I received the offer to serve again on the Saluta as second R/O. I gladly accepted, and on Thursday 29th July, signed-on again at Glasgow Docks, where she was lying. As the ship was not expected to be sailing for at least twenty-one days or so, I was able to return home for the weekend. There was a letter from Stella awaiting me when I arrived. She disclosed she was to be in Glasgow to visit family, and would be staying for a week, beginning 12th August.

I was able to get the following weekend off, and so brought Stella with me by train. It was a long and eventful journey with the engine breaking down twice. Despite this, I believe Stella quite enjoyed the short visit to

Perthshire. On 16th August, I accompanied Stella back to her extended family, before heading back on-board about 10 p.m. I learned we were to leave first thing on Wednesday morning for Loch Long, prior to sailing in convoy on Thursday. The Atlantic crossing was uneventful apart from Saturday (28th) when the escort vessels were again dropping depth charges.

We docked safely in Brooklyn, New York, on Saturday 4th September. During our stay, I accompanied the third mate to a performance of *The Merry Widow* at the Majestic Theatre. The principal singers were Jan Kiepura and Maria Eggerth. We later moved across the river to Bayonne, New Jersey, to take on our cargo of oil, before sailing off again on September 14th. Two days later, we dropped anchor at Boston in the morning before setting off again in convoy with Halifax-bound ships and reaching our destination on the 21st. After leaving Halifax a day or two later, nothing eventful occurred until the 5th and 6th of October when messages were received on both days saying U-boats were reported as being in our vicinity.

Next day (Thursday), as predicted, our escorts were again dropping depth charges. On the following afternoon around 4:15 p.m., an explosion was heard but nothing was seen. On Saturday, at 5:28 p.m., a violent explosion was heard and it transpired one of the escort vessels had been torpedoed. There was another tragedy when a spotter plane crashed. It had been launched from its 'mother' ship in an effort to locate and report on the positions of

U-boats. Unfortunately, on its return to be picked up by its mother ship, it ditched into the sea. The following days were thankfully uneventful.

At 9 p.m. on Monday 11ᵗʰ October, we broke off from the main convoy with another two ships and headed for the Clyde. Whilst I was on watch early the next morning, we were approaching the entrance boom about 5:20 a.m. when I heard loud shouting. This was followed by the stopping of the ship's engine. I immediately left the radio room and headed on deck to see what was wrong. I saw torches being directed onto the water from the ship's lower bridge. Someone shouted that Taffy Jones had fallen overboard whilst engaged in swinging in one of the lifeboats. I returned quickly to the radio room and sent out a message to all vessels in the area requesting a close watch for the missing crewman. Meanwhile, another lifeboat was lowered and crewed by a mate and five ABs.

The sea was quite choppy, there was a bitterly cold wind blowing and, to add to their troubles, the lifeboat engine refused to start. They manually put out the oars and rowed out in the direction of the life-lite, which had been dropped into the water as soon as the incident happened. When daylight came, there was no news and no sign of our lifeboat or men. Later in the morning, a passing trawler found them tied up to one of the buoys supporting the boom. They had been exhausted by their unfortunately fruitless efforts to locate poor Taffy and quite unable, in the prevailing weather conditions, to row back to Saluta. The trawler crew kindly took them on-board and towed the lifeboat back to the ship. Thereafter, we raised anchor and proceeded upriver to Loch Long where we came alongside. It was a very sad homecoming in light of the loss of a crew member.

Able seaman Taffy Jones was not a young man. He had joined Saluta at the beginning of the recent voyage in August, having apparently come out of retirement to do so. I remember him as a quiet and very likeable man. All the crew contributed to a collection for his widow and family. On 15th October, I said my farewells and left Saluta as arranged. I was placed on the shipping pool list once again.

After a few weeks at home, I had a call from the shipping pool saying the Royal Navy Auxiliary (RNA) was looking for a radio officer to take charge on a minesweeper. They explained it was not a merchant ship, so I was under no obligation to take the position. However, if I was at all interested, I should call in at their headquarters in Edinburgh for full particulars and an interview.

As a result, I travelled through to the RNA offices the following day. I was subsequently told the position was mine if I wanted it. However, on asking where the minesweeper was stationed, I was somewhat surprised to be informed it was in the Far East. In fact, it was still in the process of being built! After some consideration, I decided not to accept the position, not least due to the possibility of being stuck out there for the duration of the war.

On Wednesday 8th December, I was out when a telegram message was relayed by phone asking me to contact the Pool at Leith as soon as possible. I phoned at 9:30 a.m. the next day to be told there was a position as first R/O available on a Dutch ship lying at Cardiff, Wales. It was also explained that I was not compelled to serve on a foreign ship, but having declined the minesweeper, I felt I could not refuse. Besides, it was my first position in charge, except for the whale catcher, but there I had been on my own in any case. There was no time to waste, as I would have to get to Cardiff by noon the following day!

On phoning Perth (train) station, I learned that the first available train left at 7:30 p.m. It was some rush, but I made it. I shall not dwell on the journey by rail to Cardiff. Suffice to say, without a doubt, it was the worst journey of my life. The train was packed to overflowing, mostly with members of all the armed services. It was impossible to get any sleep whatsoever, and almost impossible to get any food or drink. To make things worse, I had a rapidly-developing head cold.

Chapter 7 – SS Winsum

Fig.26 SS Winsum

It was 3:15 p.m. on Friday 10th December when I got out at Cardiff and into a queue waiting for taxis. When I eventually got one, I wondered what on earth it was carrying on its roof.

It turned out to be a huge bag containing gas. I had met my first, and so far, only, gas-powered vehicle. My first priorities were to call at the shipping pool office, the Radio Officers' Union and finally, the offices of the Netherlands Shipping & Transport Co., to sign-on before being directed to the ship, SS Winsum, now lying at Newport. I caught the 7 p.m. train to Newport and was directed to the docks, where I finally reached the ship at 8:30 p.m. It had been a gruelling journey that lasted twenty-five hours!

When I got on-board, completely exhausted, I found that most of the crew were ashore. Fortunately, Captain de Jonghe was in his cabin, and he turned out to be a perfect gentleman. Obviously, seeing the condition I was in, he quickly had me sitting down and proceeded to mix up a strange drink for me in a large glass. The basic ingredients were 'Carnation Milk' and drinking chocolate. He showed me to my cabin, which adjoined the Radio Room, and I lost no time in getting into my bunk.

The second and third R/Os (two Welsh lads) did not arrive on-board until 11 p.m. on Saturday and both were new to the ship. There was a ruling during the war that foreign ships operating from British ports were not allowed to have any of their own nationals operate in the Radio Room. This, of course, was for security reasons. However, I personally never experienced any sign of resentment from either the Dutch or Norwegians I sailed with.

After attending convoy conferences with the captain in the morning, we left port at 4 p.m. on Christmas Eve. At only four and a half knots, the convoy speed was painfully, if not dangerously, slow. Weather on Christmas Day was good, and on the following day (Sunday), we joined a southbound convoy. Moving into the Atlantic, we encountered a heavy sea with strong winds, which remained with us for several days.

At midnight on Hogmanay, I heard Big Ben strike twelve, heralding in the New Year of nineteen forty-four. From the 3rd to the 6th of January, the weather improved daily. On the 6th, several more ships joined the convoy resulting in our progress being slowed even further, the speed of a convoy having to be that of the slowest vessel. This was intended to prevent it from being left behind and so more vulnerable to attack.

An aircraft carrier, which had been part of the convoy, sailed off on its own just as the weather deteriorated again. On Saturday morning, 8th January, we broke off from the southbound convoy and headed, with some other vessels, for the Mediterranean. After a very stormy night, we dropped anchor in Gibraltar Bay the next morning. We remained at anchor there for two weeks and it was quite an experience. There was always a good number of ships in the bay and, with the Spanish shore being quite close, security was strictly enforced.

This was primarily aimed at preventing enemy frogmen from attaching magnetic mines to the hulls of ships anchored there. To this end, small launches constantly patrolled round the ships, dropping anti-personnel depth charges, particularly in the twilight hours. I was very glad that my cabin was not below decks - depth charges coming without warning at any time are bad enough, but more so in the hours of darkness and particularly if one is sleeping below the waterline. The noise from the exploding charges made sleep virtually impossible.

I was very fortunate in that I was never in that situation in any of the ships I served on, although pretty close to it on two of them. Black-outs were strictly observed, both on ships and by the rock inhabitants. However, on occasion, numerous searchlights dotted over the rock would sweep the skies above and this was quite a sight. During the time we spent in the bay, I was fortunate enough to accompany the captain ashore on two occasions. I also managed to paint my cabin, finishing it before we moved alongside on the evening of 24th January.

Going ashore for a walk-around next morning with the first and third mates, I collected some mail from home. That evening, anti-aircraft guns on the Rock sent up a quite sensational practice barrage. Two days later, the third R/O was stopped at the dock gates and had seven bottles of wine confiscated. That is, until he was able to return with a letter of authority from the captain.

We moved back into the bay and two days later, on Tuesday 1st February, the captain and I went ashore to attend the pre-sail conference. There I met another R/O who had trained with me at Dundee Wireless College. On our way back to the ship, the captain purchased two bottles of 'Kia-Ora' orange squash and a quantity of oranges. These were placed into a paper carrier bag with string handles, which he asked me to carry. I should have guessed what would come next.

When the launch returned us to the Winsum, the captain made his way up the rope ladder, which was hanging over the side of the ship. Climbing a rope ladder is not the easiest thing to do even with the free use of your arms. Having a bulging paper bag hanging by two string handles on one's wrist makes it considerably more difficult. When I was about two-thirds of the way up, the bag and contents plunged into the sea leaving the two string-handles dangling from my wrist!

When I reached the top rail, the captain was there, waiting expectantly with his hand outstretched for his purchases. Unlike some of the crew who had witnessed the unfortunate incident, the captain had observed nothing. The captain was livid at my empty hands and his loss. The smiles of the watching seamen promptly vanished when he turned his rage on them. They received a terrible dressing-down for not having put down a rope with which to pull the bag up.

That night, we sailed in convoy from the Mediterranean along with twenty Invasion Barges. On the following Wednesday evening, we broke off from the main convoy on meeting the Freetown-bound section. We arrived at Casablanca about 1 p.m. the next day and immediately received instructions that we were to sail again at 6 p.m. We were to act as Commodore ship, with a small convoy proceeding down the Moroccan coast. We were heading to the small port of Safi where we were to load cargo. We reached Safi at 4 p.m. the next day and came alongside to commence loading immediately. Whilst we were there, I saw one of the funniest sights of my life.

To the north side of the port, there was a high, sheer cliff. Close to the edge, there must have been a road, although it was not evident to the naked eye. Early one evening, whilst standing on deck, I happened to glance at the top of the cliff. Flying along its edge, like a scene from a Western movie, was an ancient, open carriage, not drawn by a horse, but by a camel. The driver was standing up, urging the beast on with the reins in his hands, with his white robe flying straight out behind him. It was a bizarre and hilarious spectacle.

Unfortunately, there was nothing else worth seeing at Safi. One day, however, the third mate and I decided to go ashore. As we walked along the dusty street, we thought about trying to eat out. We eventually found the one and only visible eating place, which had a bar and a few bare tables. Nobody could speak or understand English. As there was only one thing on the menu, it didn't seem to matter too much. The Arab gentleman in attendance said something that sounded like '*steak*', so we said '*OK*', which he seemed to understand.

What we were eventually served was certainly not steak, at least not as we knew it. It was pale-looking but, nevertheless, reasonably edible along with the chips that accompanied it. Beyond surmising that it might be some part of a camel, we did not let our thoughts stray any further. We proceeded to consume the meal, greatly aided by the contents of a large bottle of red wine which the server had also placed on our table. The wine was quite drinkable and we decided that, as we would probably be charged for the whole bottle, we would finish it off before leaving, which proved to be no problem at all.

When the bill was presented, we noticed that we had actually been wining and dining in the impressively-named, 'Brasserie Majestic'. We immediately felt under-dressed for the occasion. The bill amounted to sixty-four francs, including a ten-percent service charge, so at least we had not been overcharged.

However, when walking back to the ship, a rather strange effect came upon me. I began to feel that my feet were off the ground, like walking on air. I have never experienced this effect since, but I have to say that I suffered no ill after-effects. Sadly, I never got back to Safi again to repeat the experience.

Fig.27 Brasserie Majestic, Safi receipt

It was midday on Tuesday 8th February when we left Safi. The following morning, as I was going for breakfast, I saw that we were passing the entrance to a buoyed channel. Shortly afterwards, fog came down and there was continued blowing of ship foghorns. I was working at the Echo meter at 10:30 a.m. when the ship shuddered heavily. Going out on deck, I saw a ship alongside and drawing away from us. At 10:45 a.m., I heard crewmen shouting that a ship was making straight for us on the port beam. Sure enough, up it came, and it was only by the grace of God that we avoided collision. Five minutes later, there was an SOS from a ship that had been hit and was now out of control.

Later, the weather cleared up and we learned that the ship which hit us initially had to return to Casablanca. Two others had to be towed in with one astern first, as she was down by the head. We followed them, but it transpired that we were the least-damaged ship.

Next day, the captain, who had gone ashore, returned with the announcement that there would be a pre-sailing conference the following day. Workmen also arrived to inspect our damage and, later that evening, bags of cement and equipment were delivered to make temporary repairs to the hull. On Friday, the captain returned ashore for the conference. The workers also left the ship as they expected us to be sailing on the captain's return. When he did return, he was accompanied by a surveyor to inspect the repairs. This resulted in the declaration that the cement-box had not been completed properly and therefore we could not sail with the convoy. Going back ashore, the surveyor and captain returned with more workmen to complete the previous repair job. Despite expecting to sail at 8:15 p.m., it wasn't until 8 a.m. the following morning before we left. This was even though the repairs remained incomplete.

At 8:30 a.m. on Sunday, we made up with a convoy which included a large number of Invasion Barges. By Tuesday, though still cloudy, the sea had improved considerably. We learned that there had been an air attack on a convoy at the weekend, at a position about two days ahead of us. Fortunately, the attackers were beaten off by planes from an Aircraft Carrier. We were told that the Carrier and five escorts were about one hundred miles ahead of us. We had to expect the possibility of an aerial attack. Fortunately, this did not occur. As we changed course towards Ireland, we were told that no plane attacks were expected now, although one attacker had been shot down in the Bay of Biscay. In other news, I picked up an unwelcome result, as the Scottish Football Team had been beaten 6 – 2 by England today.

The faster ships were now allowed to leave the convoy. Throughout the night and the following day, the weather got quite rough. Three days later, on Thursday 24th February, we dropped anchor in Loch Ewe. On instruction, we left the next day to head round the north of Scotland, then down the east coast to London. We docked there, at the Surrey Commercial Dock, on 2nd March.

When the Customs Officers came on-board, one bottle of wine and five hundred cigarettes were duly found in a drawer underneath my bunk. I was then escorted by a very self-important and imperious Customs Officer, for what seemed like miles, through the docks. We eventually reached their office, a long narrow room with about six desks along either side. I was marched through until facing the supervisory desk at the end. My 'crime' was read out to the man-in-charge. As a result, I was *'allowed'* (to quote from the receipt given to me) to pay the sum of £9, 11s & 9p as a *'compromise penalty'*. This being, *'in lieu of being proceeded against under the Customs Acts'*. Having gained my freedom from temporary incarceration, I commenced home leave on March 3rd.

I returned to the ship on Wednesday 22nd March. The next day, I had to report, with others, at the Medical Department of the Netherlands Shipping and Trading Company. We were to be vaccinated against Smallpox, and receive half-dose inoculations against Typhoid, Paratyphoid A & B and Cholera. Afterwards, and probably unadvisedly, some of us attended the Merchant Navy Club before going on to a show. On Friday, the second R/O and I set off to the Marconi Depot at East Ham for some spares and then saw a film in the evening.

Unfortunately, diary notes covering Saturday 25th March to Wednesday 29th March – when we were in Tilbury Docks – are missing. I very much regret this because I do have vivid memories of two to three days of enemy air attacks on London. The initial attacks from bombers were followed by the infamous flying bombs, or 'doodlebugs' as they were also called. These were rocket-propelled and came from specially-constructed sites on the other side of the English Channel. They flew at a fairly low altitude with an eerie screaming sound. Once their target range had been reached, the propellant cut off and the 'screaming' stopped. Then followed a deathly silence for a few seconds, until the bomb hit the ground and went off with a violent explosion. The night sky was then lit up with the flames from burning buildings.

At the time, we were tied up at a dock and close to a roadway. On the other side was a flat open area of ground upon which was sited a square-shaped battery of rocket launchers. When a raid was on-going, these were fired *en masse*. This all added to the utter bedlam that was caused by bombs, anti-aircraft guns, screaming sirens and falling shrapnel. After two nights of this, one felt very vulnerable, and inclined to think it might be safer out at sea!

This was altogether a more frightening, and tiring, experience than that when previously serving on the Peder Bogen. On that occasion, back in August 1940, we were moored in the river Mersey, off Liverpool, when that city was also being bombed on successive nights.

We received the second and final course of vaccinations on Thursday. Afterwards, we had a meal before taking in a show at the New Cross Empire Theatre. On leaving the theatre, I discovered that my left arm was so painful that

I couldn't raise it to put on my overcoat. On return to the ship, we visited the Officers' mess room where the chief and second mates were playing cards with the chief and second engineer. I sat on a chair next to the mate who, although a bit rough and ready at times, was a likeable chap. He could, however, occasionally display a somewhat bizarre sense of humour.

On enquiring how we had got on at the Medical Centre, he suddenly swung round saying to me,

"Is this the sore one?!"

He punched me right on the spot and I almost hit the roof. In an equally violent but thoughtless reaction, I stubbed out the cigarette that I was holding onto the back of his hand as it rested on the table. I quickly came to my senses and immediately thought to myself, *'what's going to happen now?'* What a relief when I realised there would be no physical response beyond the sight of the chief lying back in his chair and laughing quite uncontrollably at my reaction.

The ship moved to Northfleet to load a cargo of cement. Next day, Sunday 2nd April, I travelled by train to Worcester. I was visiting the home of a girlfriend of my younger brother John, who was serving in the RAF. One evening, we were at the local cinema when, halfway through the show, I received a shock as my name appeared on the screen with the message, *'Report back to the ship'*. This was a common, if not fool-proof system of recalling service personnel at short notice. As a result, my visit had to be cut short, albeit there was no train available until 8 a.m. next morning.

Later that same year, I would receive a Christmas card from John. This was following his deployment to the Middle East where he was then serving with Bomber Command. He would also survive the war, allowing us to be reunited prior to his emigrating permanently to the United States. He moved to Rhinelander, Wisconsin where he started a new life, and a new branch of the Anderson family, with his wife Nancy, and their sons John (Jnr), Scott, Steven and Kevin.

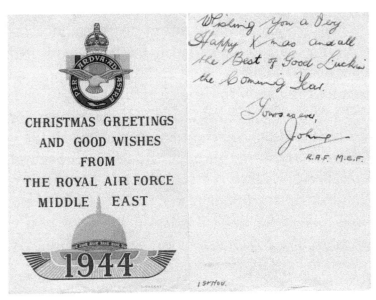

CHRISTMAS GREETINGS
AND GOOD WISHES
FROM
THE ROYAL AIR FORCE
MIDDLE EAST
1944

Fig.28 RAF Middle east 1944 Christmas Card

I managed to catch the 8 a.m. train, but then missed a connection at Charing Cross for Northfleet, with the result that I did not reach the ship until 12:45 p.m. We moved out of the dock shortly afterwards and anchored in the river until sailing out at 6:45 a.m. the next day (Friday). We docked at Methil early on Sunday 9th April. As we were to remain there until Saturday, and with the captain's permission, I set off on Tuesday to visit my parents. Having managed to see both my brother and parents, I took the chance to break off my return on Thursday to spend the night with my elder sister, Cora. She was a Queen's District Nurse, serving the communities of Glencraig and Lochore, along with her nurse colleague and friend, Chrissie MacBrayne.

When I re-joined the Winsum on Friday morning, I learned that the ship's complement had been augmented by the arrival, to the ship's cat, of six kittens. That afternoon, I attended the convoy conference with the captain, and we sailed at 7 p.m. However, during that night, I developed a terrible toothache which was to plague me all the way up the east coast and through the Pentland Firth until we reached Loch Ewe at noon on April 17th. I was very grateful to Captain de Jonghe who had made arrangements for me to visit the naval dentist on shore the next day. In the morning, I went ashore to the naval shore-base as arranged to have the offending tooth removed.

What a relief! I left the base as if walking on air. I will never forget the agony I suffered over that three-day journey from Methil, the pacing up-and-down the radio room whilst on watch. I could not concentrate on my work. When the dentist had gone and his medical assistant was seeing me off, he 'suggested' to me that a 'gift' of cigarettes to the dentist would be appreciated. Thus, on the following day, when I was back ashore attending the conference, I handed in a two-hundred pack to be given to the dentist.

We sailed out at 9:30 a.m. on Thursday 20th April, facing into a head sea and strong wind. We met up with the main convoy the following day. There were one hundred and sixteen ships in the convoy, including two with a single plane ejection launch system mounted on the bow. If, or when, these planes had to be brought into use, they could not land back on the ship. The theory was that they would land on the sea close by and be recovered by the ship's on-board crane. Given the difficulties, not least in heavy seas, I doubt if this was ever accomplished.

On Wednesday, we heard a distress message from a ship off Eire saying that she had been chased by a submarine and then torpedoed. The sea had moderated somewhat but on Sunday, there was a strong, southerly wind with some rain and fog in the morning. During that night, the ship was pitching badly in the head sea.

It was a beautiful day when May arrived, but still cold. On the following day, the sea temperature recorded one degree and we saw some icebergs in the early morning. A few hours later, both ejector planes were launched, for reasons unknown, from their respective ships. Presumably, this was for observations pertaining to U-boat activity or perhaps for spotting icebergs. The planes were still in the air when suddenly we were enveloped in fog.

Contact with one plane was lost and it was presumed to have crash-landed in the sea outwith the convoy area. The mother ship had launched one of its lifeboats, but reported later that it was also missing! The other plane was airborne for over two hours before being forced to make a crash-landing on deck, with the pilot surprisingly, and thankfully, escaping serious injury. Later in the day, the fog lessened, and at 8 p.m., the mother ship that had lost both plane and lifeboat reported that they had, unfortunately, only found and recovered the latter. They were then instructed to re-join the convoy.

Wednesday (3rd) morning dawned clear but it was still bitterly cold. Ships that were heading for Gulf ports then left the convoy. After breakfast on Thursday, the fog came down again. There was a brief clear spell after midday, but it became thick again throughout the night. Halifax-bound ships, including the two plane carriers, also broke off. Fog horns were sounding all through the night. On Friday, the Boston-bound ships withdrew from the convoy as the fog continued to come and go.

We dropped anchor in New York Harbour on Saturday about 6:30 p.m. after taking the pilot on-board some three hours earlier. We also saw both liners, Queen Mary and Queen Elizabeth, in the harbour as we arrived. On Wednesday morning, I accompanied the captain ashore to attend the pre-sail conference at 10:30 a.m. We did not get back to the ship until 5:30 p.m. due to the fact that there was only one launch provided for all convoy attendees. Taking everybody back to their respective ships, lying scattered in the harbour area, required many return trips. We happened to be near the end of the queue and, needless to say, the captain was not amused. We sailed at 10:30 p.m. the same day and headed southwards.

On Friday 12th May we heard on the radio that the allies had commenced a major offensive in Italy. It was very humid today and I saw several sharks close to the side of the ship. Over the next few days, the weather improved considerably and we were able to do a bit of sunbathing. What a change, and most welcome. After passing close to San Salvador and Cuba on the 16th and 17th respectively, we left the convoy at 2 a.m. It was Thursday morning and we proceeded independently to Kingston, Jamaica, dropping anchor at 6 p.m. In the morning, we drew alongside the wharf, and the next few days allowed some welcome sightseeing, shopping and even swimming. Whilst we were in Jamaica, the radio room equipment had to be neutralised and sealed by Customs Officers.

During our stay, some local Sailor Society officers took us by car into the country and up to the mountains. We visited an Experimental Agricultural Development Area, where we were shown around. An arranged picnic was thoroughly appreciated by all. One evening, at a hotel by the beach, the chief mate gave us quite a surprise, showing his versatility and expertise on the dance floor. Prior to our departure, we moved to the oil wharf to take on bunkers. It was 5:30 a.m. the next day when, with some regret, we left this lovely island.

Our next destination was Port au Prince in Haiti. It was on part of an island in the West Indies shared with the Dominican Republic, and close to Cuba. We arrived there on Sunday (28th) at 3:30 p.m. and dropped anchor in the harbour. Coming alongside the wharf on Monday morning, work commenced right away on loading our cargo of large sacks of local, unrefined cane sugar. Our local agent had brought some leaflets on-board including one which described a leisure club on the outskirts of the town with an outdoor swimming pool.

The Club was run as a charity with profits allocated for the benefit of poor and handicapped children. Three of us decided that we would patronise the club, so we made our way into town to look for a taxi. What we eventually located was a vintage, open-topped American car, the driver of which turned out to be a real character. As we left town along the dusty, un-made road, the driver built up speed with his foot hard down on the pedal. He then switched off the engine, allowing the car to coast along until it reduced to a walking pace. At this point, he switched on the engine once again. This was the continuing pattern of driving until we reached our destination and was apparently based on the driver's belief that he was somehow saving petrol.

The club itself was pleasant, and we thoroughly enjoyed our swim, not to mention the Planter's Rum Punch as we relaxed afterwards. 'Stirling Moss', as we christened our driver (after the famous British racing driver) was, much to our surprise, still waiting for us. On the return journey, we saw no fully-formed houses outside of the town; only the occasional cluster of shacks with corrugated-iron roofs. As we approached one of these dwellings, we noticed quite a commotion on the road, where there was much shouting and gesticulation. The central figures in the dispute were two men, one of whom was obviously a local. The other man was dressed plainly but wearing a soft Trilby-style hat and high-top leather boots. He was pushing and kicking the local man. As we slowly passed, and much to our astonishment, the man in the Trilby suddenly produced an enormous, long-barrelled pistol and brandished it at his now quite terrified victim. Our driver decided, there and then, not to wait for the finale, which also met with the approval of his passengers.

The following afternoon, we returned ashore, purchasing a few small souvenirs and postcards. During our walk-about, we came to the Presidential Palace, a heavily guarded residence which was occupied at that time by the infamous 'Papa Doc'. Retracing our steps, we stopped to have a meal at a small guest house and were directed to a table on the open veranda at the front of the building. The menu was limited but we were unanimous in our choice of French omelette with, of course, French fries.

To our surprise, the omelettes were not made individually. The proprietor duly appeared with a single, but very large platter on which lay a simply monstrous omelette, measuring some twelve to fourteen inches in diameter, and at least three inches deep, how I regretted not having my camera with me. The omelette was then deftly quartered and shared out. Any thoughts of how one would be able to consume it all were quickly dispelled with the first mouthful, as it proved to be the lightest and most enjoyable dish that one could imagine, indeed, a meal to be remembered.

We finished loading on the morning of Thursday 1st June. At 2:30 p.m., we moved to anchor in the harbour, and await sailing instructions. As soon as we dropped anchor, the bumboats arrived from the shore. Souvenirs, particularly carvings and other items made from lovely wood, were being offered for sale. After some bartering, I bought a small round-topped table with detachable folding legs with 'HAITI' carved on it, a nice oval fruit bowl and a wooden replica machete used for cutting sugar cane.

At 5 p.m., a naval escort ship arrived to escort us out to sea, where we met up with a convoy the following day. As we had failed to get papers with sailing instructions and codes before leaving Port au Prince, these were literally dropped to us from a US naval Airship, or 'Blimp', after joining the convoy.

On Monday, we heard the news that Rome had been taken, and at 12:30 a.m. the following day, a special announcement reported that Germany was claiming an invasion had taken place. Colin Thomas, the third R/O, wakened me to report that the invasion had indeed been confirmed. This was, of course, the historically important 6th of June D-Day Landing on the French Brittany coast. No doubt this would have involved the Invasion Barges we had earlier carried as cargo.

Over the next few days, the weather was not so good, and it steadily grew colder, so on Wednesday, I was surprised to see a large turtle close to the ship.

We dropped anchor at Staten Island in the early afternoon of Friday 9th June. After going ashore, the captain returned to announce that we would not be sailing out until 23rd June. Next day, we moved upriver and dropped anchor again. During the night, we experienced a very severe storm with thunder, lightning and torrential rain. We lay at anchor for nearly two weeks without any incident of note happening. That is, apart from the night I returned too late for the boatman to take me out to the ship. I had to seek a bed at the nearest, but very dubious, accommodation where I could have had company, had I so desired.

At last, our wait was over, the captain and I were taken ashore at 8 a.m. to attend the pre-sail conference. We learned that there were eighty-four ships in the convoy with another forty-eight expected to join later from the south. Once again, only one launch was provided to return attendees to their respective ships. The captain and

I had to wait until 4:50 p.m. in the quayside queue and, as the Winsum was one of the ships furthest away, it was 7:30 p.m. before we got back on board. By this time, I can say that our captain was not the happiest of men as we sailed out at 10 p.m. into a cloudy night and with a slight sea running. Our voyage across the North Atlantic was uneventful and in generally moderate weather though dull, and this continued as we drew near to the Scottish mainland.

At 1:30 p.m. on Sunday 9th July, we broke off from the convoy and headed for Loch Ewe, where we anchored at 7 p.m. the following day to a real Scottish welcome - rain and mist. We left the following night at 8 p.m. and headed, once again, round the north of the country to the east coast. However, when I was called on Thursday morning, I was given the most welcome piece of news,

"We are going to Dundee!"

We arrived there at midnight and dropped anchor in the River Tay. The captain allowed me to travel home on the Saturday with instructions to return on Tuesday. This I did, but only to be told I could go back home again and would be informed when I had to return. I re-joined the ship at Leith on Tuesday 20th July but only two days later, due to ongoing delays, I was once again back home. I recall hearing on the news at this time that the Allies were now in Romania and Bulgaria. On 2nd August, I heard that Finland had 'asked' Germany to withdraw their troops from their land!

I finally returned to the ship on Wednesday 23rd August and we sailed the next morning at 7 a.m. After adjusting the compass, we proceeded to Methil where we docked in the afternoon. Having taken on our cargo of coal, we set off again at 7:30 p.m. on Sunday and headed north, in convoy. The following day was cold and dull, and, during the night, I experienced a very strong feeling ... a sense of unease. It felt as if 'something was on' or about to happen. Yet, nothing did happen, at least not to us.

I have never been able to associate that strong premonition with any incident occurring at that same time. All I can say is that, in all my life, I have never experienced any other similar feeling. To add to the mystery, my diary for the following day reads, '8:15 a.m. told PRO – BEL'. I believe this signified the abbreviation of two words but I have been unable to decipher these ever since.

(Editor's Note: Taking up the search for any significant event(s) occurring around this time that might explain the author's premonition, it was identified that 'Operation Goodwood' was ongoing in his general North Sea vicinity. This was the operation to destroy the German battleship 'Tirpitz'. Despite repeated RAF bombing raids, including a final unsuccessful attempt on the 29th of August, 'Tirpitz' remained a serious threat to Allied shipping.

Another consideration, although only speculation, was the possible involvement of the author's brother John, a wireless operator & gunner for Bomber Command. Having come so close to many threats over the past four years, this one and only premonition remains a mystery. Unfortunately, the diary entry 'PRO BEL' remains similarly unexplained. 'BEL' could refer to 'Belgium.' On 29th August, Montgomery's 2nd Army commenced its advance on Brussels.)

A week after rejoining the ship, we dropped anchor in Loch Ewe on Friday 1st September. After I attended the pre-sail conference at 10:30 p.m., we promptly sailed out again. We joined the main Atlantic convoy the next day, thus taking the total complement of ships up to one hundred and sixty-five. By Sunday, the weather had become very rough, with loose or unattached objects flying about. The cabin shared by the second and third R/Os got washed out by a heavy sea. Thankfully, things calmed down later in the evening.

On Monday, almost exactly five years since war had been declared, we heard that the Allies were now in Holland. This was great news for the captain and the mainly Dutch crew. Tuesday turned out to be a clear day. Although the sea was not quite so heavy, the ship was still rolling. At 8 p.m., a distress message was heard from a ship, saying that she had been hit by a torpedo. Similarly, on the following morning, another ship was torpedoed near Cape Race, in our vicinity.

On Thursday 7th September, we had clear weather. At about 10:25 a.m., depth charges were being dropped by our escorts, which continued the following day. The sea was calm, but we had fog throughout the night and thick patches during the day. On Sunday, we heard news that

Mr Churchill was in Canada, and a hurricane had hit the West Indies. Hopefully, these were not omens of things to come. Enemy activity reports continued to be received into the following week, including a submarine sighting in the vicinity of Cape Hatteras. In addition, the radio room was receiving Admiralty messages. Weather reports suggested that we might get the hurricane now in the Cape Hatteras area. During the day, we picked up a total of nine distress calls from ships in that region. Fog came down in the afternoon and we heard that Atlantic City in the USA had been badly damaged by the hurricane, now said to be heading for Nova Scotia.

On Friday 15th September, the captain had me roused at 6 a.m. to take a bearing because of fog. Because of a previous incident, he simply would not rely on anyone else to take bearings on our DF. At midday, the fog lifted and a buoy was sighted from the bridge lying dead ahead. I thankfully accepted the compliment on the accuracy of the bearing. We had arrived safely in Sydney, Nova Scotia.

At 1 p.m., the local Sydney Radio Station put out a message telling school children not to return to school in the afternoon because of hurricane fears. Shortly afterwards, a gale sprang up and we lifted anchor to tie up alongside right away. Going ashore the next day, it was terribly warm as I called in at the local agent's office for mail. I was particularly pleased to be rewarded with letters from home. Come Sunday, we were glad that we had only experienced the tail-end of the hurricane. We also heard news at this time that Paratroopers and gliders had landed in Holland.

On Tuesday evening, the captain threw a party in the saloon to which he had invited the local agent, ship chandler and some of their staff. It was expected, of course, that the senior ship's officers would attend. After a good meal with ample refreshment, records were played on the gramophone to which some danced. Others chatted away into the night, at the end of which I believe the guests had enjoyed their visit.

On Wednesday evening, a young lady from the agent's office, who had attended the party, invited me to come for tea at her parent's home, where I met the family. Helen was a very nice girl and I greatly appreciated her very kind hospitality. The only 'hiccup' I can remember occurred when I was being shown the family photograph album. On turning a page, I suddenly found myself staring at a very close-up photo of an infant, lying in a coffin and staring up at me. It had been taken at a wake. It was certainly a different photo experience for me.

We sailed out of Sydney, Nova Scotia, on Friday 22 September, having taken on bunkers the day before. The weather was misty and rainy and I was asked to take bearings on several occasions. There were only nine ships in the convoy. The Winsum rolled about very badly throughout the night, with the result that I did not get much sleep. Throughout Saturday, we were a straggler in the convoy and still tossing badly. At night, it became much colder and the Aurora Borealis was clearly visible.

During the day, I had been asked again to take more bearings and this continued through Sunday morning and afternoon whilst we were in the St. Lawrence River estuary. About 5 p.m., and still a straggler, we turned off from the course of the convoy and approached our destination of Mont Louis in the Province of Quebec. It was a small village consisting of a few houses with a simple wooden wharf stretching out from the shore.

No pilot was provided, so we had to make the approach without assistance. In doing so, unfortunately, we struck the wharf as we came alongside. This gave a fright to nearly all the local population who had, by this time, gathered to greet our arrival. After we had tied up, several of the reception party came on board to welcome us. This was, in part, explained when, to our surprise, they announced that Winsum was the first ship to visit Mont Louis in two years. One of their party was the Corporal in charge of the local army radio station. He promptly invited the captain and myself to visit the station. We did so and were treated to coffee and cake.

The next morning, a few of us took a walk to the village and, as we passed the radio station, we were hailed and asked in for a chat. Later that afternoon, I had a surprise visit from Corporal Joe who said he had come to invite me for dinner with him, the landlady of his lodgings and her husband. Needless to say, I accepted and, in any case, it was evident that they were all keen to have new company to talk to.

I cannot remember details of the meal, apart from the fact that for the first time in my life, I had eaten corn-on-the-cob, having been freshly picked from a plot outside the house. After dinner, we chatted well into the night, and eventually, I said that I would have to go back to the ship.

"Not at all," was the response.

"You can stay here," and they refused to take no for an answer.

Next day, Tuesday, the captain announced that he wanted to throw a party for the locals on Sunday evening. He instructed the third mate and me to cooperate with Joe in making a list of those likely to accept. This we did. Before leaving, Joe told me that he and two others were travelling the next morning to Gaspe with a friend who had a business there. I was welcome to join them and had to be ready at 8:30 a.m. as it was a long journey. How could I refuse?

After leaving Joe, I met another visitor to the area. He was either a Geologist or a Surveyor and he asked where I came from. On my reply, 'Scotland', he countered,

"Yes, but where in Scotland?"

I replied that it was only a small village near Perth so he would likely never have heard of it. With a knowing smile, he explained,

"My ancestors came from Pitcairngreen."

This being another small village and only five short miles from my own home, it was indeed a small world.

On Wednesday, Joe collected me as promised, and we transferred into a large American saloon car owned by his friend. We set off down the long but quiet coast road to Gaspe, which lay at the point of the Gaspe Peninsula looking across the Gulf of St. Lawrence to Newfoundland. The journey on the dusty road took more than three hours. There was little habitation on the way, with just the odd house seen now and again. It was most interesting for me, however, and two memories stand out in my mind. One was a large porcupine which crossed the road in front of us, and the other was a placard by the roadside which read, *'See Where the First Torpedo Hit the North American Shore'* – *'Price to View, Only 50 Cents'*.

When we arrived at Gaspe, Joe's friend left to attend to his business. The rest of us proceeded to a large naval shore station where Joe was well known. As a result, there was no difficulty getting through the well-guarded entrance gate. After our visit, we found a lovely restaurant for lunch where we were reunited with Joe's businessman friend, who was sitting with another acquaintance. After an excellent meal, it was time for us to leave. It was to some embarrassment, however, that Joe's friend insisted on paying for our meal. I was quite overwhelmed by his generosity.

I was feeling quite tired by the time we arrived back at Mont Louis, but Joe persuaded me to have dinner with him again. It turned out there was a surprise waiting for Joe. He was given a message that he and two others were to be drafted to serve elsewhere. I returned to the ship soon after dinner ready for a good sleep, as another visit had been arranged for us the following morning.

Thursday's visit was again by car, but this time we were turning off the road to Gaspe and travelling up a mountain track to the top of the 1,277 metre-high, Mont Jacques Cartier, the highest mountain in Eastern Canada. On this occasion, the second and third R/Os were also invited with two others, a local man and his daughter. Our visit was to an Army Air Force-operated radio station on the top of the mountain. The ground on either side of the track was heavily forested with fairly mature trees for most of the climb. On reaching the top, however, it was only tundra.

We made only one stop on the upward journey, about halfway through the forest. This was to call at a cabin occupied by a Forest Ranger and situated by the side of the track. It was constructed from rough-sawn timber but beautifully finished both outside and in. It reminded me of the cabins I used to see in cowboy and western films when I was young, albeit without the up-to-date embellishments.

On reaching the radio station at the top of the mountain, we received a very warm welcome. We were then given a tour of the building and an inspection of their radio equipment. We then sat down to a massive meal.

The main course was either moose or caribou steaks of enormous size. These magnificent wild animals were not difficult to come by in such an isolated area and we were delighted to see one walking across the tundra. After expressing our thanks and appreciation for our hosts' hospitality, we set off down the mountain after a most memorable day.

However, a very unfortunate incident happened, which introduced a sour note to the proceedings. Whilst coming down the very steep incline, there was a point where the track was standing quite high above the forest floor on our left. It was a sheer drop. The second R/O, who was sitting in the back, gave out a loud yell and opened the car door. He thought it was a great joke, but it scared the living daylights out of the driver, his daughter and myself who were sitting in the front. It could have ended very badly had we careered off the track and plunged down the embankment to the forest below. The culprit was duly made aware of our feelings about such stupidity. The rest of the journey was completed in silence.

On our return from the mountain, Joe accompanied us to the ship and dined with us there. Thereafter, he took the captain ashore to attend to some business at the local notary's office. They returned a short time later, accompanied by two other lads from the station, and willingly accepted our offer of a beer. However, when we produced cans, they were amazed, never having heard of beer being available in anything other than bottles. They even wanted the empties as souvenirs. Joe insisted on giving me a small knife which he had made from a .303 calibre bullet and cartridge, and which I still possess over fifty years later.

I accompanied the lads back to the station and it was after midnight when I returned on board the Winsum. I had been invited to stay the night ashore but, after some thought, I decided not to accept the offer. Little did I know that this would turn out to be a providential decision.

At 6 a.m. on Friday, I was awakened by the sound of rough weather so I got up, dressed and was on deck about 8:30 a.m. I was astonished by the scene of heavy seas breaking over the wharf. The captain, mates and deckhands were in sea boots, working frantically on the securing ropes, fore and aft. Leaving the saloon after our delayed breakfast, the captain asked me to go ashore to telephone the authorities at Gaspe regarding our situation. I was to report that, if conditions got any worse, we would sever our mooring ropes. Several, in fact, had already broken. I hurried to my cabin to put on a coat and sea boots. On returning to the main deck, I found that the gangway had been taken on board as it was being smashed up by the high seas. The captain decided to cancel any attempt to go ashore. He was going ahead to sever the ropes, whilst the ship was now lying with her bow to the shore.

Once the head ropes had been cut with axes, the engine room was given the order, *'full astern'*. The ship swung out and round to the other side of the wharf as it was still being held by the stern ropes. As a result, there was some damage to the structure. With the ship now facing out to sea, and the stern ropes finally severed, the *'full ahead'* order was given. There was all round relief as we moved safely out and into the estuary. It was revealed that we had a large dent amidships, caused by impact with the end of the wharf when we swung around. Altogether, we were relatively lucky as it could have resulted in a more serious situation. I was asked to take a bearing at 2 p.m. and the second mate said he would call me at 4 p.m. for another. However, I found that the weather was clearing, and by supper time, it was a beautiful night, with land visible on both sides of the river.

We docked at Quebec City at 8 p.m. on Saturday, the last day of September. The captain came to talk with me about our very abrupt departure from Mont Louis. His very personal and revealing thoughts came as an extremely pleasant surprise to me. Indeed, I felt complimented by his confiding his inner thoughts to me. As a result, I sent a letter right away to the boys at the radio station expressing regret over our unexpected departure and the forced cancellation of the captain's farewell.

I also reminded Joe that I still had his army torch, which he had lent to me for my return to the ship on the previous night. A reply reached me sometime later from Marcel, one of the boys at the station. They also expressed their regret at our having to leave so suddenly, adding that they had come to the wharf with a message for the captain.

However, it had been completely impossible to reach the ship because of the seas breaking over the wharf. He said that Joe had already been transferred but had said I was to keep the torch as a souvenir from him.

The next paragraph in his letter stated that two hours after we left, the storm passed and was, *'all nice and quiet on the sea'*. He also added, *'It is too bad you could not stay here because your girl was very sorry to see that you had left in the morning!'* I was flattered as the trip up the mountain was the only occasion I recall being in the girl's company. I did remember a race back to the car when we left the radio station on the mountain when I stumbled and fell. She came to my rescue and took my hand until we reached the car, so I was conscious of her being a very good-looking young lady. Now, if only the storm had not come, and the captain's party had taken place, well, at least I might have recalled her name!

Whilst we were at Mont Louis, our steward got permission to visit a girlfriend who, at his request, had travelled up to Quebec from New York. He was supposed to have re-joined the ship at Mont Louis on Monday. The captain gave me the address of their apartment and asked me to go ashore to let him know that we had moved up the river to Quebec. The steward had previously told us of his girlfriend and he had a photograph in his cabin of this attractive young lady. I duly set off and was quite looking forward to meeting her. When I arrived at the address, the lady herself answered the door ... and, did I get a surprise!

My face must have been a study when I saw this vision of advancing years in her dressing gown standing before me. Her blonde hair was not natural, and although her make-up was plentifully applied, it failed to hide a well-lined face. After giving my message, I couldn't get away quickly enough. I was extremely glad that I had not seen the steward personally. As expected, when I returned to the ship, my fellow officers were eager to hear what I thought of the lady in question. They found it difficult to believe my story and the aforesaid description. In the end, it was decided that the photograph was either her daughter or another girlfriend altogether!

During the rest of the week, I was able to get ashore most days to see the sights. These included the famous Château Frontenac, where Mr Churchill had his famous meeting with Allied leaders. Whilst not being able to take on our full cargo of timber at Mont Louis, this was remedied at Quebec, when we replenished our bunkers at the oil wharf.

We sailed out at midday on Saturday 7th October in dull and squally conditions. The convoy consisted of only twelve ships. By Monday, and because of dreadful weather, we found ourselves separated from the others, and unable to locate the pilot boat we were expected to meet. Eventually, we found it in a sheltered location. On Tuesday, I was called from my bunk to take a bearing, and this was to continue at regular intervals, right through the day and into next morning. I then learned from the bridge that we had only travelled eighty-eight miles in the last twenty-four hours. On Wednesday, the sea was calm but fog persisted and I continued to take bearings all day until 2 a.m. the next morning. Six hours later, we were finally able to anchor at Sydney in clear weather. We came alongside the wharf on Saturday and, once again, the captain announced that he was throwing a party that night. One of the guests was a fellow Scot, Captain McKinnon, whose ship was also in port. I had quite a chat with him, and I believe he had Glasgow connections.

I was ashore for the usual convoy conference on Wednesday 18th October and was pleasantly surprised to meet a fellow R/O who had trained with me at Dundee Wireless College. We left Sydney at 7:30 a.m. the next day in nice weather, and on Friday, we joined another convoy.

We heard on the news today that America had invaded the Philippines. The good weather had continued through to Saturday, and on that day, I was surprised to hear the BBC news quite clearly on the medium waveband. That weekend, however, the weather began to deteriorate and we had a problem with rain coming through the deckhead in the radio room. By the following weekend, we were into fog and I was told that during Saturday and Sunday, we had only been making six and a half knots.

At 7 a.m. on Tuesday morning, the last day of October, the ships bound for Loch Ewe broke off from the convoy. At 7 p.m., and again at 8 p.m., I had to take bearings. Then, at 9 p.m., the light situated at Tory Island on the northwest coast of Ireland was sighted from the bridge. I had turned in about 2 a.m. on Wednesday (1ˢᵗ November) when there was the sound of an explosion on a destroyer escort vessel, but we did not learn the cause of this.

The Clyde-bound ships had left us sometime during that night, and those for Liverpool on Wednesday night. I was kept busy taking bearings until 2 a.m. on Thursday as we approached the Bristol Channel. We subsequently anchored off Barry, moved to Weston Bay next day, and finally docked at Newport on Saturday. On Sunday, I left the ship for what turned out to be an extra-long spell of leave.

A letter arrived from Colin Thomas, third R/O, on 3ʳᵈ December informing me that the ship was not entering dry-dock until the 6ᵗʰ, and it was possible that repairs would not be completed until early January 1945. The reason for the delay was understood to be caused by a dispute between the Dutch and UK authorities regarding the extent of the repairs required to be carried out. Indeed, it was midday on Monday 8ᵗʰ January when a call came for me to return to the Winsum.

I left home at 7:30 p.m. that night, in a blinding snowstorm, to catch the train in Perth. I did not reach the ship until 3:30 p.m. the following afternoon. To my surprise, I found that she was still in dry dock. However, we did move out the following Monday as the ship was due to be fumigated the next day. The crew had to move ashore to live in guest houses from Monday to Wednesday.

Our landlady was a bit of a harridan, and I was not sorry to return to Winsum, despite the lingering smell of fumes which remained for some days.

We finally sailed out at 11 p.m. on Sunday 20th when snow was falling, and we headed for the river Mersey. We picked up the pilot at the Liverpool Bar on Monday morning at 11 a.m. and proceeded upriver to anchor at 2.30 p.m. We then upped anchor again at 6:15 p.m. and passed into the Manchester Ship Canal. When the Canal pilot came on board at the first lock, I was amazed to recognize him as Hugh MacPherson. He was the former chief officer of the fated Peder Bogen, the very same man who had suffered an injury to his foot whilst involved in a gun practice exercise. We tied up for the night, proceeding again next morning after our mast tops had been removed to facilitate passing under a bridge. Unfortunately, we had to tie up again at 4 p.m. because of fog, but were able to continue the next day to our destination of Partington.

With the captain's permission, I set off for home on Thursday morning to catch the 4 p.m. train from Manchester to Perth. It was 2:30 a.m. the next day before I reached Perth. As there were no taxis to be had, I was compelled to walk the seven miles home, giving my parents an early wakening. On Monday, the day before I was to return to the ship, snow was falling and I decided to lay up my brother John's Ford 8 saloon. I had, more or less, fallen heir to it after he was called up some two or three years earlier as an RAF gunner/wireless operator.

Next morning, I found that another foot of snow had fallen overnight. Fortunately, I had arranged for Betty, from Lawson's Garage next door, to pick me up at 8 a.m. Betty was the Garage office clerkess, and also drove the school bus. This was used, not only for scholars, but also for transporting POWs to and from their camp to work at local farms. Little did we know then, that some four and a half years later, Betty and I would be man and wife.

Fig.29 'Betty', the Author's future wife

When we got to Perth, I learned that the train leaving at 9 a.m. should have left at 8:25 p.m. the previous night. It had been held up by snow on its journey down from the north. I had to change trains at Carlisle, where I had to wait for two hours before catching the train to Manchester, arriving at 8 p.m. instead of 4:45 p.m. as scheduled. I was fortunate to have the aid of a policeman who got a taxi to take me to the ship, depositing me there at 9 p.m.

Imagine my disbelief when I found that all my rush and worry had been unnecessary as the cargo of coal still remained on board, and our departure was not imminent. It was Wednesday 31st January before we moved further up the Canal to Irlam, where the cargo was discharged for the steel works there, before returning the following day to our previous berth.

On Monday 5th February, the captain persuaded me to accompany him to the home of a 'friend' for the purpose of repairing a radio. This was despite my protestations that I neither had the test meters nor parts that might be necessary to affect a repair. I was to find out that there was more to the invitation than met the eye. When we arrived at the friend's home, I found that there was an officer of one of His Majesty's Forces there. Awkwardly, it transpired he was the friend's husband. He was returning to his base that evening after being home on weekend leave. I sensed that I was to be the pawn in this affair when the captain and I were shown to the bedroom we were to occupy that night. On returning downstairs, I found that the captain had insisted that he and I would accompany the loving wife to the station with her husband and witness the latter's departure.

On return to the house, we were served supper, and, when the hostess was clearing away the dishes, I noticed the captain giving her a playful smack on her rear quarters. I was then informed that the twosome would withdraw to the lounge, *'to play records'*, and so I could investigate the broken radio in peace and without any interruption – how considerate, I thought. Needless to say, I found that the radio was not out of order and did function. Perhaps not as well as it might have, but without a test-meter or spares, there was nothing much I could do.

I did wish that there might have been a fuse blown, or a break in a lead, so that my visit could have had some justification, but that was not to be. I had to accept it as yet another experience of life. There was, of course, little evidence of surprise exhibited by the twosome when I gave my verdict on the radio, and this naturally did not surprise me either.

I said my goodnights and retired upstairs to bed. I heard footsteps shortly afterwards and the captain entered the room but it was a fleeting visit. He simply reached an arm to the back of the door, and without a word, swiftly removed his dressing gown and departed. I cannot say that I was disappointed.

After breakfast the next morning, I returned to the ship on my own. On the train, I got into conversation with an elderly fellow traveller. I was very interested to learn that he was an ex-W/Op (wireless operator). He had visited South Georgia in the Antarctic, back in 1926, when he served on board a ship named SS Overdale. He was equally interested to hear that my first trip to sea had taken me there when serving on a Whaling Expedition in 1939-40. On returning to the ship, I found that loading was not yet completed due to some wagons having gone missing.

Loading was finally completed on Thursday and we sailed out at 3 p.m., stopping for the night at Latchford near Warrington. As to our cargo, I can't remember what it was called, but it might have simply been coal dross, as it had that appearance, and the dust covered everything in sight. Next morning, I left the ship at 8.30 a.m. accompanied by third R/O Colin Thomas. We took the train to Liverpool where we spent the day. I then attended the usual pre-sail conference in the evening, before rejoining the ship at Eastham where she was now lying. We moved out of the Canal the following day to anchor for the night, and then sailed from the Mersey at 7:30 a.m. on Sunday 11th.

We soon encountered rough seas. Within twenty-four hours of sailing, depth charges were already being dropped by our escorts. Tuesday was a calmer day and the convoy split, with the American-bound ships continuing westwards, and our lot turning south. Towards the end of the week, we experienced fog, but Sunday was a beautiful, clear day.

This continued into Monday when we received an RRRR message, which signified that an enemy Armed Raider vessel had been sighted in a given position of 32.07N, 13.24W. We later came upon an empty ship survival raft which was then checked by one of the corvette escorts, who found that it had come from a ship which had been torpedoed two days earlier. We passed Gibraltar at 6:45 p.m. and entered the Mediterranean. Afterwards, we left the convoy, and, on the following day, dropped anchor in shallow water off Oran.

In accordance with instructions received, we upped anchor at 2:15 p.m. on Wednesday 21st February. Sailing close to the Algerian shore for a time, we then turned off on a straight course for Ajaccio on the island of Corsica. We arrived at Ajaccio on Saturday morning in beautiful weather, dropping anchor to await further instructions. The captain was taken ashore later, and on his return, he said that a mine had exploded there the previous day, killing twenty people. We sailed at 8:30 a.m. the next morning in a convoy composed of only four ships and one escort. At night, we heard news that Allied warships had been shelling the French Riviera.

We arrived at Marseilles on Monday at 8:15 a.m. and left again next morning at 7:30 a.m. for our final destination, the small port of Sète. The convoy now consisted of only three ships, and we had to proceed in line-astern formation through a cleared passage in a minefield. We reached the quaint harbour at 4:15 p.m. I believe that when France surrendered, several senior Army Officers made their way to Sète, where they were picked up by submarine and taken to safety.

A start was made on unloading our cargo on Wednesday when we had a visit from the captain and second engineer of the SS Baron Douglas. Both were fellow Scots, the engineer being a native of Spittalfield, Perthshire, which was also my birthplace. His name, I think, was Lucas. We had to wait until Monday 5th March before the captain was able to get French francs, and so enabled us to go ashore with some money in our pockets.

When we made our way into town, we got quite a shock. Most of the shops were closed, and the large covered marketplace contained only empty tables; apart from one. This only held a few pieces of fly-ridden red meat lying unprotected on display. It was mind-boggling to witness the scene and realise the plight of the few inhabitants left, and to wonder how they had survived. We were quite sickened by the desperate situation there and made our way back to the ship. As a result, we had every sympathy for the ladies who had been patrolling constantly up and down the dock, trying to chat up all and sundry, ever since our arrival.

I made one last visit ashore the next day in a vain effort to use up the francs I had asked for. To my surprise, I found what appeared to be a jeweller's shop which was open. In the window were displayed only a few small items of jewellery, a small clock and some pieces of Limoges porcelain. My eye was caught by a rather attractively decorated vase. I purchased the Limoges items and the clock. I managed to get the vase home in one piece and my mother was quite delighted with her present from abroad, which now lies in my own home and is often admired.

Unloading was completed on Thursday 8th March and we moved to the outer harbour. We lay there until our departure at 8 a.m. on Saturday, when we retraced our steps to Marseilles. We arrived at 4 p.m. and then departed six hours later into a strong wind. The weather then improved on Monday, and, in excellent conditions, we passed close to another convoy of twenty ships coming from Oran and bound for Marseilles. Next day, we passed another convoy inward bound and an American destroyer ordered us to alter course to 300 degrees. It was apparently thought that we had either not altered course to a sufficient degree, or not acted promptly enough for our American friends, as they then threatened to *'fire'* on us ... some friends.

We arrived at Gibraltar at 8:30 a.m. on Wednesday, a day earlier than expected, and dropped anchor in the bay. We left at 1 a.m. the next morning heading for the Port of Huelva in Spain, which, during the war, was known to house enemy agents. Because of this, a very ingenious plot was contrived and executed to fool the Germans. It turned out to be a complete success which made a major contribution to bringing forward the day of final victory.

The top secret plot (later known as Operation Mincemeat) involved using the dead body of a man who had no identification or (as it was believed at that time) any known relatives. He was dressed in a Senior Officer's uniform, and in his possession were 'Very Secret' papers which ostensibly showed extremely sensitive troop movements and invasion plans. The body was then taken by submarine to a spot off the Spanish coast where it was put overboard. Calculations, plus information received, had indicated that currents would probably take the body to the shore in the vicinity of Huelva, and this proved to be the case.

When the body was discovered (probably by paid informers searching the beaches), all the evidence was obtained by the German High Command, who were completely fooled by it all and altered their defence strategy accordingly, and to their subsequent detriment.

Fig.30 Huelva Port Shore Pass

We docked at Huelva at 4:30 p.m. but were not able to get ashore as we had neither official passes nor pesetas! On Friday morning, the money was available, but still no passes. We waited until 2:30 p.m. but there was no sign of the passes, so we decided to take the risk of going without, and in this we were lucky. There was more to be seen in the shops here, and on this occasion, I bought yet another clock, ladies' stockings and a leather interwoven belt for myself, which I still have to this day.

Whilst in town, a young Spanish lad came up to us and introduced himself as Manuel. He could speak pretty good English and offered his services as our interpreter. He turned out to be an exceptionally nice, honest lad. On Saturday morning, I accompanied the chief engineer ashore as he wanted to make some purchases. We returned later in the afternoon with Jones, the second R/O. We met Manuel again and he took us for a walk to the outskirts of town, where we saw inhabited cave dwellings dug into the side of a cliff. It was quite unbelievable.

It became obvious that this part of Spain had not recovered from the effects of their Civil War and we were shown ponds which used to be full of frogs but now had none. They had all been consumed during the conflict as there was little else to eat. It must have been a dreadful existence.

I can recount a story from one of the engineers on a previous ship who told me of how he had been in a Spanish port during that previous conflict. On coming on deck for a breather one day he was horrified by what he witnessed. A frail, pathetic-looking mother was accompanied by a young daughter of about six or seven years of age and equally bedraggled. She was looking up at the ship and begging for a loaf of bread, for which she was offering her own child in return. Words fail me now when I think of her being in such a dire situation.

Another incident happened when we were in town with Manuel. Whilst sitting on a bench, he told us that fear still existed because of their dreaded secret police. At one point, he asked us not to speak too loudly as a man, who had come to sit nearby, was obviously watching us with some interest. Manuel was clearly worried in case he was thought to be speaking ill of, or complaining about, the State.

Before returning to the ship, we took Manuel for a meal and on our way to the café, I noticed an attractive filigree, gold-plated ladies' bracelet in a jewellery shop window. I thought it would be right for Betty's 21st birthday on 7th April. I returned to the ship alone at 8:30 p.m., with Jones deciding to remain with Manuel. Next morning, he informed me that Manuel had introduced him to three girls, and it had been arranged for us to meet them tonight.

Going ashore at 6:30 p.m. to meet Manuel and the girls meant that we missed dinner aboard ship. This was due to the fact that the old man had invited the Manager of the Rio Tinto Mine, together with his wife and daughter, for dinner at 6 p.m. However, they had still not arrived by the time I left. I had the excuse, if needed, of having a previous appointment. The aforementioned mine was the source of our cargo, which we were about to load. On meeting Manuel and the three girls, we had a walk until a shower of rain came on. As a result, we retreated to the nearest café. The girls were very nice and could speak a little English, but Manuel had to assist a good deal with interpretation. We soon realised that Spanish parental control was quite strict, and, without Manuel's presence, we would have been unable to enjoy their company.

Our four friends said their goodbyes at half past ten and returned to their homes. On our way back to Winsum, we called at a bar, where we met some lads from another ship, the SS Baron Tweedmouth. In the course of conversation, it came out that one of them knew a friend of mine from Perth called Robin Keay. We had not only attended Perth Academy together, but he had also been instrumental in my following him to Dundee Wireless College, where we both trained as R/Os.

Monday 19th March was a local holiday and all the shops were closed. As a result, we did not go ashore until evening, when we once again met the girls and Manuel. It was then decided that we would go to the cinema, which turned out to be something of a disaster for us. Presented with Spanish translation, it was a German propaganda film! However, we sat it out for our friends' sake. We said our last farewells to our four friends at 10 p.m. On our journey back to the ship, we joined the chief and second engineers, whom he noticed sitting in a bar.

We finished loading the next day and sailed from Huelva at 6:15 p.m. We were met outside Spanish territorial waters sometime between 8 and 9 p.m. by a naval escort. It supplied us with further instructions and a course to follow. I did not get much sleep that night as there was quite a gale blowing and a rough sea. Because of the nature of the cargo, being heavy ore, the ship was lying very low in the water and accordingly, was shuddering very badly, which did not promote good sleep.

We reached Gibraltar at 6:30 p.m. on Wednesday and dropped anchor in the bay. The weather was now cold and very dull. On Thursday, we had a naval diver inspecting our hull to see if there were any magnetic mines attached. I received one letter from home, and several more on Friday. Throughout Saturday, a fighter plane kept sweeping over the many ships lying in the bay, and we were informed that enemy frogmen had again been swimming out from the nearby Spanish shore and attaching mines to ships. Our hull was again inspected by a diver and this was repeated the next day. Throughout the night, anti-personnel depth charges were also being dropped in an effort to combat this problem.

After heavy rain throughout the night, Monday turned into a beautiful day. In the morning, before going ashore with the captain to attend the Conference, I saw the SS Baron Tweedmouth arriving from Huelva. Whilst ashore, I managed to get my hair cut and collect more letters, including a missing one from Betty. We lifted anchor and sailed out between 3 and 4 p.m.

We were enjoying better weather on Tuesday, but the ship was still rolling heavily. We heard the news today that Argentina had decided to join the allies' cause. Next day, we were sailing close to the coast and had been left with only one escort ship. Then, by the end of the week, we were experiencing cold and dull weather with rougher seas but were glad to see more escorts arriving on Saturday. Ships bound for the English Channel broke away from the convoy on Sunday 1ˢᵗ April, and I had to start taking bearings again.

We arrived at Weymouth about noon on Monday, with the captain attending a conference alone, later that evening. We sailed the next morning, and, after a further delay at Southend, we finally arrived at Ipswich at 1:30 p.m. on Thursday. A pilot arrived, but only to take us into the river entrance, where we would anchor. Finally docking at 6 p.m. on Friday, I ordered a taxi for 6 a.m. the following day.

Today was the 7ᵗʰ of April and Betty's 21ˢᵗ birthday. The taxi ordered for 6 a.m. did not arrive, but I managed to catch a bus to the station and get a seat on the 7:30 a.m. train to York. With having to change trains at Edinburgh as well, it was after 9 p.m. before I reached Perth. I then took a taxi out to Methven and Betty's home, where my arrival caused some surprise. My own home was no longer in Methven, as my mother and father had moved only two days earlier, to live with my elder sister. She was now based at Fowlis Wester, about seven miles further west. My stay at Methven, therefore, was necessarily brief. I had to phone my sister to let her know I was back and ask her to come in her car to collect me before my parents retired for the night. On Thursday, I received a call saying I had to be back on board by early morning on Saturday 14ᵗʰ April.

At 7:15 p.m. on Friday, Charlie Gordon from the Methven Garage arrived with a taxi so that I could catch the 8:20 p.m. train from Perth. The train arrived in London at

9:10 a.m. on Saturday. By further train and taxi journeys, I eventually reached the ship at 12:45 p.m. This was cutting it neat as we left the dock only forty-five minutes later to adjust compasses and then to anchor.

We upped anchor at 11 a.m. on Monday, in nice though slightly hazy conditions, and joined a passing convoy. Unfortunately, my original diary notes for the following day are incomplete, except for, *'we came alongside at 5:30 p.m.* and, *'I was disappointed that the loading of our cargo, by means of a chute, had started immediately'*. I am unable, therefore, to name the port or the nature of the cargo, but from my calculations of the times of the journeys to and from this port, I believe that it must have been in the Tyne area. Loading completed, we sailed out again at 6 p.m. on Wednesday which had turned out to be a beautiful warm day. We arrived in Methil the following morning around 5:30 a.m. We learned later that we were not likely to be sailing for at least six days, so, on Saturday, the captain allowed me to go home for the weekend.

Monday 23rd April dawned bright and beautiful so I was delighted to receive an early phone call telling me that I needn't return until Wednesday. Leaving home after lunch in dull and rainy weather, I was on board Winsum again by 5 p.m. I was surprised to find a letter awaiting me from Stella in Ireland as I had not heard from her for some considerable time. The contents of the letter gave me quite a shock and were quite upsetting. In essence, I was berated for having stopped writing, and without giving any reason for doing so. This, of course, was not true as

I had several letters unanswered, and I myself had been wondering why. Although I received some letters during the war, which had small pieces cut out, they were few in number, and I never had any evidence whatsoever of a letter being confiscated. I could understand perhaps one letter being lost, if, for instance, a ship carrying our mail had been sunk, but in any case, not all my letters were sent from abroad. Although I replied to the letter and explained that I had not stopped writing, I sadly received no further reply. On a previous occasion, when I was home on long leave, I had applied to the immigration authorities for a permit to visit Northern Ireland. They replied that this was not possible at that particular time. As to my final conclusion, I have to reluctantly think that my letters were intercepted and possibly withheld from Stella. Her mother, whom I met in Moville, was an extremely nice and friendly lady, but sadly, she died a year or so afterwards. This left Stella to look after her father and much younger sisters which was to be a huge responsibility. That, and being of different religious faiths, although not an issue for either of us, may have been an issue for her family. Stella Maris (Star of the Sea) – I shall always remember her as a very gentle and caring young lady.

I attended the pre-sail conference on Friday 27th, and we sailed out at midnight. It had become very cold the next day when we heard the news of the death of the Italian leader, Benito Mussolini. After a very rough night on Sunday, we were unable to make it through the Pentland Firth in daylight. The captain decided to alter course for the Stronsay Firth, eventually dropping anchor in the bay near Lerwick in heavy, driving snow. We remained at anchor until 1:30 p.m. on Tuesday 1st May, and it was shortly after midnight that we then heard the tumultuous news of the death of Adolf Hitler!

Immediately, this then reminded me of the Jewish owner of a shop in Curaçao in the Dutch West Indies who said to me two or three years earlier,

"When the war is over, Hitler should be put in a cage and taken all over the world, so that we can all spit on him!"

Wednesday 2nd May 1945 was another momentous day. After reaching Loch Ewe, with the background of snow-clad mountains, we heard the great news that Berlin had been taken. Joseph Goebbels (Nazi Propaganda Minister) had committed suicide, Gerd Von Rundstedt (Nazi Wehrmacht Field Marshall) had been captured and the German Forces in Italy had surrendered.

After going ashore to attend the convoy conference that same afternoon, we sailed out the next morning at 6:30 a.m. It was a lovely day and a very calm passage through the Minch. In the news today was the story that Hamburg had been declared an 'open city' having been entered by Allied troops. The city of Rangoon, in Burma, had also been taken.

We joined with another convoy in the early hours on Friday 4th May, making fifty-four ships in all. At around 8:30 p.m. that evening, the old man burst into the saloon apparently in a great rage, shouting in staccato,

"What's the matter?" ... *"What's happened?"* ... *"Why did it fade out?"* ... *"Is it surrender?"*

The questions were all directed at me, and I began to think that he had taken a brainstorm. However, after he had calmed down a bit, it at last transpired what happened. He had been listening on his own radio to the Dutch news from London. Reception quality was poor and he had only been able to pick out the occasional word from the announcement that, *'German Forces in Holland and Denmark were to capitulate as from 8 a.m. the next day'.*

Saturday 5th May - Holland is liberated! There was not as much excitement as I would have anticipated amongst the Dutch crew. That is, apart from the captain. He called us to the saloon for a celebration drink and made a somewhat embarrassed reference to his display the previous evening. The Commodore of the convoy sent a message to all Dutch ships saying to hoist their ensign at their foremast.

On Sunday, I heard Land's End radio calling St. Peter Port (Guernsey) in the Channel Isles with a message, requesting their *'surrender'*! Also heard was a message from Prague in Czechoslovakia asking the allies for assistance.

(Editor's note: The original telegraph message handwritten on a Marconigram and received at '10:15 GMT on Monday 6th May '45' by the author ('A.A.') reads as follows:

"TO PETERPORT from GLD (LANDSEND RADIO).

FROM ADMIRAL PLYMOUTH 061119B TO COMMANDER GERMAN FORCES CHANNEL ISLANDS":-

"THIS IS THE STATION OF THE G.O.C. IN C SOUTHERN COMMAND WHO IS AUTHORISED BY THE SUPREME ALLIED COMMANDER TO RECEIVE YOUR UNCONDITIONAL SURRENDER STOP

LISTENING WATCH WILL BE MAINTAINED BY DAY BETWEEN 0900 AND 2000 HOURS GREENWICH MEAN TIME ON FREQUENCY 4982 KCS PER SECOND AND BY NIGHT BETWEEN 2000 AND 0900 GREENWICH MEAN TIME ON FREQUENCY 1570 KCPS STOP

THE LINK CALL SIGN TO BE USED WILL BE JEIB STOP

SHOULD THE GERMAN COMMANDER WISH TO SEND A MESSAGE TO G.O.C. IN C. SOUTHERN COMMAND HE WILL COMMUNICATE USING THE FREQUENCY AND CALL SIGN ABOVE STOP

ACKNOWLEDGE RECEIPT OF THIS MESSAGE. 061119B."

Today, Monday 7th May, the Germans signed their General Surrender and, importantly for us, Admiral Doenitz recalled all U-boats. It was also revealed that Goebbels, his wife and family had all died together from poisoning. On the following day, I heard speeches given by His Majesty the King and Prime Minister Churchill. A message was also intercepted, reporting the sighting of U-boats on the surface at 49.00 N, 28.00 W.

When listening to the BBC News at midnight, I heard the announcer say at the end,

"... I am now giving the first weather forecast of peace!", which was,

"Local thunderstorms over most of the country, with bright intervals."

I continued listening to broadcasts of people celebrating in the streets of the UK until 2 a.m. and felt very much out of it!

(Editor note: The following Marconigram in two parts from 'Admiralty' marked 'Immediate' was received and handwritten by the author (A.A.) at '1220 GMT 8ᵗʰ MAY 1945', was sent to 'BAMS AREAS 1a, 1b, 3a, 3b, 3c, 5a, 7a, 7b, 7c, 9a, 9b', and read as follows:

'THE GERMAN HIGH COMMAND HAS BEEN DIRECTED TO GIVE THE FOLLOWING SURRENDER ORDERS TO U-BOATS STOP

(a) TO REMAIN ON THE SURFACE FLYING A LARGE BLACK OR BLUE FLAG BY DAY and BURNING NAVIGATION LIGHTS BY NIGHT STOP

(b) TO MAKE FOR SPECIFIED PORTS UNDER ALLIED CONTROL STOP

(c) TO REPORT THEIR POSITION IN PLAIN LANGUAGE ON 500 KC/S EVERY EIGHT HOURS STOP

U-BOATS APPARENTLY COMPLYING WITH THESE INSTRUCTIONS ARE NOT TO BE ATTACKED BUT

SHOULD BE GIVEN A WIDE BERTH STOP

'CONTINUATION OF 081100Z:-'

'W/T REPORTS OF SUCH SIGHTING ARE TO BE MADE IN PLAIN LANGUAGE IN THE FOLLOWING FORM

(a) NUMBER OF U-BOATS

(b) POSITION

(c) ESTIMATED COURSE

(d) ESTIMATED SPEED

IF HOWEVER U-BOATS COMMIT A HOSTILE ACT OR OTHERWISE DISREGARD THOSE ORDERS REPORTS ARE TO BE MADE BY NORMAL DISTRESS PROCEDURE AND ALL APPROPRIATE DEFENCE MEASURES TAKEN 081100Z'

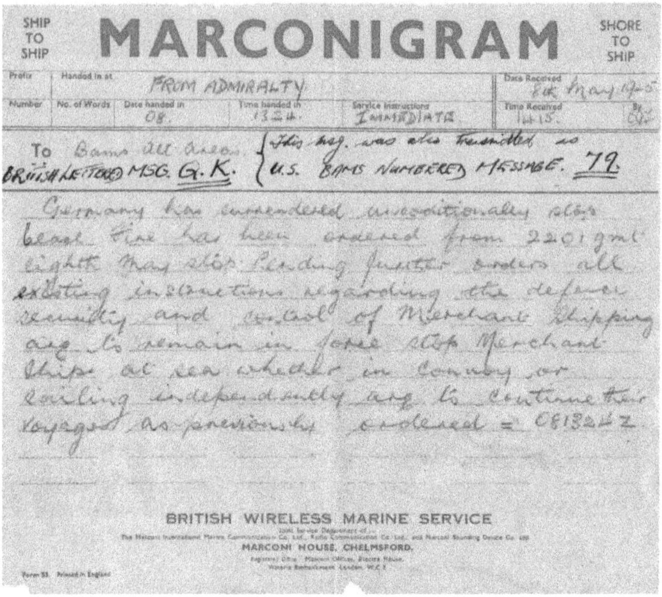

SHIP TO SHIP

MARCONIGRAM

SHORE TO SHIP

Prefix	Handed in at				Date Received
	FROM ADMIRALTY				8th May 1945
Number	No. of Words	Date handed in	Time handed in	Service Instructions	Time Received / By
		08.	1324.	IMMEDIATE	1415.

To Bams all areas. { This msg. was also transmitted as
BRITISH LETTERED MSG. G.K. { U.S. BAMS NUMBERED MESSAGE. 79.

Germany has surrendered unconditionally stop Cease fire has been ordered from 2201 gmt eighth May stop Pending further orders all existing instructions regarding the defence security and control of Merchant Shipping are to remain in force stop Merchant Ships at sea whether in Convoy or sailing independently are to continue their voyages as previously ordered = 081324Z

BRITISH WIRELESS MARINE SERVICE

MARCONI HOUSE, CHELMSFORD.

Fig.31 Admiralty Message of German Surrender

Less than two hours later, the above Marconigram message, also marked 'Immediate', from Admiralty to 'BAMS all areas' was similarly received at `1415' as follows:

'Germany has surrendered unconditionally stop

Ceasefire has been ordered from 2201 gmt eighth May stop

Pending further orders all existing instructions regarding the defence security and control of Merchant Shipping are to remain in force stop

Merchant ships at sea whether in convoy or sailing independently are to continue their voyages as previously ordered = 081324Z'

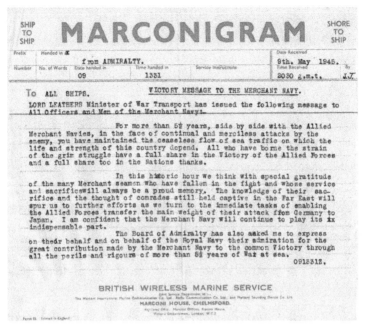

Fig.32 Admiralty Victory Message to Merchant Navy

On Wednesday 9th May 1945, a message to all members of the merchant navy from the Minister for War Transport, Lord Leathers, was received.

(Editor note: The above typed Marconigram message, received at '2030 g.m.t. 9th May 1945' from 'ADMIRALTY' to 'ALL SHIPS' read as follows:

'VICTORY MESSAGE TO THE MERCHANT NAVY'

'LORD LEATHERS Minister of War Transport has issued the following message to All Officers and Men of the Merchant Navy:-'

'For more than 5 1/2 years, side by side with the Allied Merchant Navies, in the face of continual and merciless attacks

*by the enemy, you have maintained the ceaseless flow of sea
traffic on which the life and strength of this country depend.
All who have borne this strain of the grim struggle have a full
share in the Victory of the Allied Forces and a full share too in
the Nation's thanks.*

*In this historic hour, we think with special gratitude of the
many Merchant seamen who have fallen in the fight and whose
service and sacrifice will always be a proud memory. The
knowledge of their sacrifice and the thought of comrades still
held captive in the Far East will spur us to further efforts as
we turn to the immediate tasks of enabling the Allied Forces
to transfer the main weight of their attack from Germany to
Japan. I am confident that the Merchant Navy will continue to
play its indispensable part.*

*The Board of Admiralty has also asked me to express on their
behalf, and on the behalf of the Royal Navy, their admiration
for the great contribution made by the Merchant Navy to the
common Victory through all the perils and rigours of more
than 5 ½ years of war at sea. 091331Z.')*

Another message came from an unidentified vessel,
saying a U-boat had been sighted on the surface at 37N,
47W and heading west. It was also announced today
that airborne troops had entered Oslo. We saw some
improvement in the weather on Thursday, but although
the sea was not quite so rough, the ship was still jumping
about. We learned on 10th May that the SS Avondale Park
had been torpedoed on the day of surrender off the northeast coast. Sadly, two crewmen were killed!

Other news received today included: Surrender of both the German Forces in the Channel Islands and Quisling in Norway; the island of Crete had been taken; the first U-boat to surrender arrived in Weymouth, and six others had been observed from the air, flying flags of surrender. It was also confirmed that some German troops were still holding out against the Russian forces in Czechoslovakia and finally, Winston Churchill announced that the basic petrol ration would be restored in thirty days' time.

(Editor's note: a further Marconigram radiotelegraphy message (below), retained, and intercepted by the author (A.A.) at '11.30 G.M.T. 11th MAY 1945' was sent, 'by GERMAN SUBMARINE 190' to 'VCE (CAPE RACE RADIO)' and read:

'I WILL GIVE YOU MY PLACE IN GERMAN –

I WILL GIVE MY POSITION IN GERMAN –

STANDORT   42 GRAD 30 MIN NORD

*   42 GRAD 30 MIN WEST –*

KURS NEUN NULL GRAD – FAHRT NEUN SEEMEILEN.'

'AT 1131 G.M.T. VCE SENT – R O.K. PLEASE STAND BY ON 500 KCS

AT 1132 G.M.T. U-BOAT SENT – I HAVE UNDERSTAND YOU.'

'RECEIVED by -   A. Anderson, Chief Radio Officer'

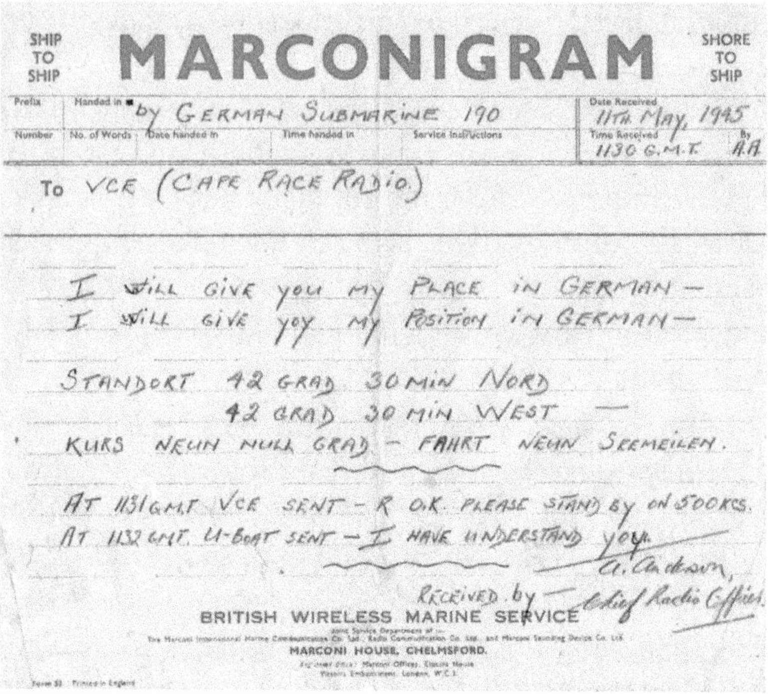

Fig.33 Author's Receipt of U-190 Surrender Message

A (modern) German to English translation for the above provides the following:

'LOCATION 42 DEGREES 30 MINUTES NORTH
42 DEGREES 30 MINUTES WEST – COURSE NINE
ZERO DEGREES – DRIVE NINE MILES'

(Editor's note: On transmission of their coordinates, U-boat U-190 subsequently surrendered the same day (Friday 11th) to the Canadian HMCS Victoriaville off Cape Race, Newfoundland.

Fig.34 U-190 Surrender taken by HMCS Victoriaville

Saturday 12th May brought dull and rainy weather with fog, not to mention a heavy sea running onto our port bow. As a result, the Winsum was rolling very badly. Thankfully, Sunday was a better day with the sea somewhat subdued. A Liberator aircraft was flying around, and we received a chilling reminder in a message saying, *'Not to relax vigilance until all U-boats had been accounted for.'* A further message gave a warning of icebergs in our vicinity.

On Monday afternoon, we entered the Newfoundland Banks and, by 6 p.m., we were into dense fog. The ship's horns were constantly sounded until 5 a.m. on Tuesday, by which time we had cleared the lower end of the Banks. The notorious fog experienced in the Newfoundland Banks is caused by the interaction between the Labrador currents from the north meeting the Gulf Stream from the south. I read a report in an American magazine describing how a United States Coast Guard vessel had sat across the opposing Gulf Stream and Labrador currents. On taking temperature measurements in the water at the bow and stern of the two-hundred-foot-long vessel, the results showed a temperature difference of twenty-two degrees.

The St. Lawrence section of the convoy, which included us, broke off on Wednesday. More fog in the afternoon, resulted in my having to take bearings again on the DF. We heard today that a total of thirty-seven U-boats had now surrendered.

The sea was like glass on Thursday and it was quite clear to the horizon where it became hazy. The mate called me out to see a most remarkable sight, or rather, two remarkable sights. Abeam of us there was an inverted mirage of St. Paul Island on the coast of Newfoundland 95 miles away. Slightly on our port beam, a similar mirage appeared off Cape Breton Island. They were quite unbelievably distinct and an experience to remember.

Our convoy dispersed at 11 p.m. that night and I later heard an American news report stating that a Japanese submarine had been captured off Newfoundland and two of the crew had committed Hara-Kiri. It was also claimed that Japanese submarines had operated in the Atlantic last summer. Another report stated that the Cruiser HMS Curaçao had been sunk two and a half years ago with the loss of 340 lives. It was apparently cut in two by the liner Queen Mary and sank in only seven minutes!

(Editor's note: The Curaçao, originally a WWI vessel, was converted during WWII as an anti-aircraft cruiser and was eventually assigned to the Western Approaches. On 2nd October 1942, a zig-zagging tactic alongside the Queen Mary, then carrying US Troops, led to what became known as the Curaçao Tragedy, but was not made public until the end of the war.)

In the early hours on Friday, I heard a US weather report for 18th May stating that there was a belt of cold polar air over Canada and the east-coast states. This made me wonder if that had some bearing on the refraction effects seen yesterday. I had been instructed to take DF bearings every hour all afternoon and into the early evening. When I saw that the coast was visible at 8 p.m., I asked the old man if he still required a bearing, but he replied '*no*'.

As the coast was still visible at 9 p.m., I didn't take a bearing, but when the fog came down again at 10:10 p.m., I took one then handed it over. To my surprise, the captain was in a rage and, despite my earlier clarification, asked why he had not received one at 9 o'clock. I took another bearing at 11:10 p.m. and on taking it to the bridge, I discovered that the coast was visible to them, and they had already taken a visual bearing. The captain checked the bearing I had given and graciously confirmed that it was correct. I think he regretted his previous outburst.

At 7:45 p.m. on Saturday, the pilot arrived on board. As it was such a beautiful night, I remained on deck until we finally docked at 1:15 a.m. at Quebec. It turned out to be a lovely, warm and sunny day, which the locals said was the first decent day for the past month. Unloading of cargo commenced first thing in the morning, and this was done by massive, fast-operating grabs, which unloaded directly into waiting lorries. As a result, the job was completed by evening. During Monday afternoon, we moved to another berth. The following day, I accompanied the chief engineer ashore but was thereafter compelled to stay on board all evening because of violent thunderstorms with winds of seventy-five miles per hour. However, I was ashore most days, walking around, having a meal and going to the cinema.

On Monday 28th May, we received letters from home which were eagerly opened. Also on this day, we heard the good news that convoys were to be stopped, and ships in the North Atlantic were no longer required to be blacked out at night. In the evening, it began raining heavily and continued until midday on Tuesday. I had arranged to go ashore in the afternoon with the two chiefs (mate and engineer) but called it off as I wanted to write a reply home.

However, I did go ashore in the evening with the third mate, and saw the film, 'A Song to Remember'. The weather became very cold, and on Friday, it was announced on the local radio station that fifteen inches of snow had fallen in

North Quebec the previous day. At 7:17 a.m. on Saturday, I was awakened by noises in the radio room which adjoined my cabin. While investigating, I found one of the shipyard workers there. He seemed to be genuine, claiming he was, *only having a look around*'.

There were several fellow Scots among the workers. They had been recruited at the beginning of the war, because of a shortage of skilled shipyard workers in Canada. One of them was a very nice and friendly chap who invited us to his home for a chat any time. His name was Robertson. That afternoon, the third mate and I visited the nearby town of Levis and then Quebec itself. We had a meal at the popular Peking Restaurant before returning on board at 7:17 p.m. By this time, I had a severe headache and was feeling sick, so I retired to bed.

Sunday was a better day and I decided to take up the invitation to visit the Robertson household early that evening. I got a very warm welcome from Mr Robertson who introduced me to his wife and daughter, Joan. It turned out to be a very happy evening indeed, with lots of laughter. It was obvious that they very much enjoyed the company of a fellow countryman. At one point, we all took to the streets to watch a very colourful religious procession. This was accompanied by bands and the throwing down of masses of flowers in the path of the procession. When I got to my bunk that night, I found that some joker had distributed pebbles between the mattress and sheet.

We had to get two inoculations carried out ashore. I cannot remember what they were, but I believe it was done in consideration of Winsum's impending return to Holland after a six-year absence. Whilst ashore, we saw a notice in a window announcing that it was now possible to send cables abroad without censorship, so we took the opportunity and sent our *'Greetings from Quebec'*.

Thus, for the first time during the war, we were able to inform our families of our location. I also took the opportunity to buy a radio valve and other items. These were to enable me to repair a second-hand Philco car radio, which I had purchased in Levis, but which was not working to my satisfaction. With the spares, I was able to fix the radio which turned out to be a very successful purchase. Although old, and built like a tank, it was a terrific performer, giving great satisfaction for many years to me, and then to a friend Jimmy Pirie, a butcher in Newtyle. I learned it then passed to a farmer who later bought Jimmy's car, complete with radio.

We did our best to fill our days with trips ashore, which usually meant spending money on treats. On Monday afternoon, I was invited by Thomas, and Veldhuis, the third mate, to join them in some cake and ice cream they had purchased ashore. This must have somehow energised me, as I began to paint the radio room shortly afterwards, completing the job that night.

On Wednesday evening, the third mate suggested we go and call on the Robertson household again and, of course, we received another warm welcome. I remained amazed at the very real and genuine generosity we received from complete strangers on such visits. We could only hope we were able to provide some enjoyable conversation in return with our stories of home.

I decided on Saturday that I would get myself ashore again, this time to travel to the nearby township of Lauzon, in order to get a haircut. However, as I was leaving the ship, a Lloyd's surveyor, who was also leaving the ship, offered me a lift in his car to Quebec. I decided to accept, but in some respects, this proved to be an unfortunate decision. Still eager to fulfil my original aim, I had to wait for nearly one and a half hours for my haircut. It was performed by a French Canadian and the delay was no doubt due to his unhidden, nationalistic feelings. However, I remained determined to see it through to the end and not walk out. After all, not everyone was happy to entertain me.

On Monday 11th June, with great excitement, the second engineer became the first Dutch crew member to receive a letter from his family in Holland. It was his first news of home in nearly six years and contained the information that he was now a grandfather. Also on this day, Thomas and Jones were the victims of a hoax played on them by the second and third mates.

The mates had called on the pair in their mess room handing over typewritten, official-looking papers. They were told these had been delivered on board by the Authorities. They purported to be orders telling them they were being transferred immediately to take up new duties in the Far East. They were asked to sign their names at the foot of the instruction, signifying their acknowledgement of, and agreement to, the order. The mates were looking for me as soon as I returned on board, and gleefully told me of their ploy and its initial success. They added that Jones, immediately on signing, had rushed off to pack his case. I was very glad that I was not present, as they would surely suspect that I was involved in the incident.

Next morning, I was wakened at a quarter past seven by Mr Robertson, who said, much to my surprise, that he had heard that we were to leave today and wanted to say cheerio. Whilst I believed that the ship would move out of dry-dock today, I had no information about leaving for good. He then left saying that Mrs Robertson and their daughter Joan would be disappointed if they missed saying goodbye to the third mate and myself.

When it was confirmed that we would not be leaving today, I phoned the Robertsons and said that we would try and visit tonight if at all possible. Thus, after dinner, when I made my way to the deck, I found to my surprise that I couldn't get off the ship as the gangway had been removed. The third mate appeared and told me that although he was on duty and unable to come, he had a way to get me off the ship and onto the dock. He got the operator of the large crane and grab, who had removed the gangway, to swing the grab on-board allowing me to jump in, and that was that.

Later that evening at the Robertson household, we all got a surprise when the third mate made his very unexpected appearance. The ship had moved out of dry-dock and he had then persuaded the second mate to agree to the tossing of a coin in order to decide who would stay on duty. It was midnight before we were able to say our goodbyes to our very good friends, with our repeated and earnest appreciation of their hospitality. We also called in at the Old Homestead hostelry on our way back to the Winsum where we arrived at 1:30 a.m.

On Wednesday, I decided to have a quick trip ashore and purchased a jacket and a holdall. When I returned on-board, I saw the chief engineer standing by the ship's rail. It was evident that he was not in one of his better moods, as no greetings were exchanged. I later learned that he had good reason to be upset. He had unfortunately been sick over the rail and, in the process, had parted company with his dentures!

We took on oil bunkers in the afternoon and although the pilot came on board at 6 p.m., we had to wait another hour or so for the late arrival of the Compass Adjuster. We then moved into the river to enable the adjustments to be made. It was 10 p.m. before this was completed, so allowing us to sail. We dropped off the pilot the next day at 12:30 p.m. It was announced on the radio that Joachim von Ribbentrop, Nazi Germany's Minister of Foreign Affairs, had been captured.

We picked up another pilot at 6 p.m. on Friday to take us upriver to Campbellton, New Brunswick. We arrived two hours later, but some time elapsed before we got tied up at the wharf. Next morning, I accompanied the chief engineer ashore in order to do some shopping. When the captain returned in the afternoon, he announced that we had been invited to join the locals at a dance that night, with transport being provided. Thus, at 8:30 p.m. a bus arrived, complete with locals and the band. It soon became apparent that the local males were not too keen on our presence. This back-fired on them by earning the wrath of the young ladies for their bad-mannered display. The bus returned to town about 1:30 a.m. on Sunday when two of the girls spoke to Colin Thomas and me before saying goodnight. They provided their phone numbers, saying that they would be pleased to show us around if we so desired. Their names were Kay and Huddie.

I missed breakfast, having slept in that morning, but was wakened by the uncommon sound of female voices at 9:15 a.m. However, I did not get out of my bunk to investigate the source, and no one volunteered to make me any the wiser. In the afternoon, I walked into town and met Kay as arranged. I asked if Thomas and I could meet her and Huddie on Monday evening, and this was agreed. As I began retracing my steps, a dreadful shower of rain began. There was no taxi to be found, with the result that I had to walk all the way back to the ship, soaked to the skin.

Next evening, as planned, we met the two girls and, after a short walk and some discussion, it was decided that we would go to the cinema to see "Thirty Seconds over Tokyo". The next day was dull and wet but receiving letters from home was a nice compensation.

On Wednesday, I headed ashore to do a little shopping as we were to be moving downriver to Carleton-sur-Mer to complete the loading of our cargo of wood. This was due to there being an insufficient depth of water at Campbellton to allow a full cargo to be taken on. Carleton was situated by the side of the bay into which the river Restigouche flowed. We tied up at the wharf there less than two hours after leaving Campbellton.

Carleton was a small but very attractive village situated on the coastal road and a popular holiday resort. There were a few small hotels and guest houses and one café. Going ashore that evening, we were passing one of the hotels when we were hailed by a group of people sitting on the veranda. They were exceptionally friendly and pressed us to look in for a chat on our return from our walk. This we did and sat with them awhile, before getting back on board about 11 p.m.

On Thursday afternoon, I called in at the Post Office after going ashore to stretch my legs. I encountered an elderly man in front of one of the local hotels. He could certainly talk. I could not get away from him as he continued in full flow for a full half hour before I finally made an excuse about returning to work. In the evening,

I was persuaded by Veldhuis and Thomas to accompany them for a return trip ashore for coffee and sandwiches.

After two unsuccessful efforts at the first two establishments, we were finally able to have our requirements fulfilled at the Carleton Hotel. Whilst there, we tried to phone Kay but there was no reply. Then, when it was time to return on board, the heavens opened up with a torrential downpour. We were fortunate to get a local taxi to do the needful. However, when I got to the radio Room, I found to my dismay that a leaking deckhead had resulted in the radio transmitters being drenched – what a day.

Friday was cold and dull, with the result that I didn't go ashore until early evening. On doing so, I found myself once again sitting with our visitor friends, whose names I believe were Wilson and Collins. I asked to be excused whilst I made a phone call to Kay, but despite getting through, she was out. By the time I tried to phone again, I was being teased relentlessly by one of the ladies. She was not going to be content until she learned the name of the girl concerned.

Of course, in the end, it transpired that she knew her, and spoke very highly of her as well. Fortunately, on my second attempt, I managed to speak to Kay, and, on my return to the table, I was greeted with,

"Well! … what did she say?"

When I announced that Thomas and I were invited to come up to Campbellton the next day, there then erupted great hilarity from the audience.

We caught the 9 a.m. bus which arrived in Campbellton at 11:30 a.m. This was an issue when we realised it was actually 10:30 a.m., as there was an hour of time difference between the two towns. After having a meal, we sat in a park for a time before meeting the other girls at Kay's home. We then learned that they were taking us to an Indian Reservation for a picnic. It was a lovely day and we all thoroughly enjoyed the outing.

After seeing the two girls safely home, we returned to the hotel where we had earlier booked a room for two nights. We didn't rise for breakfast on Sunday morning, but took a short walk at 11:30 a.m. Thereafter, we parted company, as I was going to Kay's home for lunch and Thomas was going to Huddie's. It was another lovely day so we had a cycle run in the afternoon, followed by a short walk in the evening. Thereafter, we saw the girls home and returned to our hotel.

Monday brought us a reminder that accidents were never far away when we learned the sad news that two R/Os had lost their lives yesterday. They had been trying to swim ashore from a ship anchored off Dalhousie on the opposite shore of the bay.

On Wednesday 27th June, I was ashore in the afternoon having had my hair cut when Thomas joined me. As we walked past the St. Louis Hotel, two of the ladies there hailed us and took us into the dining room for a glass of beer. On our way back to the ship, we heard voices behind us. On turning around, we realised that it was the lady from the hotel who had wanted to see the photos from our visit to Campbellton. We chatted briefly until it became evident that they dearly wished to see the ship, so we obliged and gave them a brief look around.

I returned ashore in the evening with my two assistant R/Os, Jones and Thomas. We found the café packed, so Thomas and I decided to go for a walk but Jones, who seemed distracted, did not accompany us. On our return to the café sometime later, we saw an empty table so decided to stay for a coffee and a sandwich. It was quieter so Anita, the daughter of the proprietor, joined me in conversation. A mess steward from the ship arrived later and sat with us until closing time when he and I made our way back on board.

Next day, I learned from the lads on the ship that they had been teasing the fourth engineer quite shamelessly about Anita. Apparently, he had quite a fancy for her, however, they told him he had a rival in the chief Sparks; that being me. I was told this by his tormentors with great glee when I sat down to dinner. Their 'victim', it transpired, had been rushing ashore earlier, without partaking of the evening meal. The weather had cleared somewhat after dinner and, going ashore about a quarter past eight, I looked in at the café.

Jones joined me later and then Anita's brother arrived with his girlfriend and her brother. When the café closed, Anita's brother took us all out for a short drive in his car, before returning Jones and me to the ship. They wouldn't stay but were pleased to have a look round the ship before returning home. As they descended the steps from my cabin to the main deck, Anita let the others go first. She must have enjoyed her visit as she turned round, placed both hands on my shoulders, and kissed me, before following behind the others; a very nice gesture from an exceptionally nice young lady. I realised how well we had been received by a variety of Canadian hosts, some passing acquaintances and some becoming firm friends, given our extended stay.

Friday was a beautiful day and I was again ashore in the afternoon to see if there was any mail but without success. The mail train had not arrived and was now five hours overdue. I walked along to the café and had a chat with Anita and her friend Jeanette, before returning to the ship. Returning ashore again in the evening, I called once again at the Post Office, but still no arrival of the mail train.

On passing the St. Louis Hotel, I was inevitably hailed and summoned to sit awhile by our friends. Shortly afterwards, two figures walked past and turned out to be Anita and Jeanette. I excused myself to join them, followed by laughter ringing in my ears from those whom I had left in such a hurry. The girls were only going to the garage before returning to the café, but on our way back, we managed to 'rescue' Jones from the St. Louis, where he had been snared after I left.

I was later driven back to Winsum with Anita and two friends. They had driven away when I suddenly remembered that I had not paid my bill. Going ashore the next morning, I made sure I paid my bill to Anita, which she had also completely forgotten about. On my way back, the old man from the Post Office hailed me and handed over two letters to take back to the ship. Once aboard, I received two pieces of news in return. The captain had gone away to Campbellton for the weekend, and a truck driver had called to present a kitten to the ship. It was a slow news day.

The St. Louis Hotel was flying the Canadian Flag on Sunday which, being the 1st of July, was celebrated as Dominion Day. Thomas and Veldhuis were off to fish in the bay but I decided not to join them in their venture. On Monday, I made my usual call at the Post Office and then on to the café to meet with Anita and Jeanette. The old man arrived back in the early evening from his trip to Campbellton with a number of new-found friends in tow. He duly announced that he was entertaining them with one of his usual onboard parties, and we all had to attend. I think it was appreciated and enjoyed by everyone present. The old man always initiated proceedings at his parties with the same opening and accented words -

"Laydees and Schentlemen ... I am not much of a speecher ..."

This reminds me of another occasion when I returned on-board Winsum and was collared by the third engineer who was in a somewhat agitated state. He proceeded to tell me of a conversation he had with another member of the crew. In the course of their chat, the latter had said something which was, apparently, somewhat offensive to the third.

"What do you think of that 'Sparks'?", he enquired.

Before I could reply, he drew himself up to his full stature, looked me straight in the eye, and firmly declared in his best English,

"I told him that I was disgusting!"

With regard to those two observations, it highlighted the difficulties that can be encountered when translating or speaking in a tongue which is foreign to your own. I have to say that I have nothing but praise and full admiration for the captain(s), officers and crew of the Winsum for the way in which they conversed quite freely in English with the British crew members. They were, in retrospect, too good to us. It might have been better for us to have overcome laziness and tried to learn the Dutch language more earnestly. By the end of my two years of service on Winsum, I was, nevertheless, able to get the gist of some of the conversation in Dutch when it was used at meals in the saloon, but I could not converse in the language, bar a few words and phrases.

I shall never forget my embarrassment when we returned to Amsterdam in October 1945. I was standing with my two assistants on deck when the first party of officials from the owner's agents came on board. There wasn't a mate around at the time, and the leader of the group came up to us, and said in Dutch,

"Where is the captain?"

After a hesitant pause, I stammered out,

"Hij ist te boven,"

which, to the best of my knowledge meant, he is above, the captain's room and adjoining saloon being on the upper deck. To my surprise, the official wasn't taken aback by my vain attempt at Dutch. In fact, he must have assumed some fluency on my part and continued to address me with a full torrent in Dutch, none of which I could understand. This fairly took the wind out of my sails and I had to very hurriedly confess that I was not a native of these shores and, very obviously, not fluent in the language!

On Tuesday morning, I wakened to find a crab in my cabin, which I later found out to be the work of the third mate. He was the resident joker and prone to such surprises, as had been common on other vessels. I was relieved that he hadn't put it under the bedclothes as he had done with pebbles.

Going ashore in the afternoon, I called at the café, which was very quiet at the time, allowing Anita to take a break and sit outside. I sat with her, and in the course of conversation, she very hesitantly enquired if we were able to buy 'drink' on the ship. To this, of course, my answer was 'no' and that only the captain was in possession of alcohol. It was then disclosed that Anita's mother was very partial to a drop of 'Bols' Gin on occasion. Of course, at that time, Canada was almost dry, with the issue of alcohol being strictly rationed.

Before we left Quebec, I learned that a State Office was open on a certain day for a limited period of time, when a ration of alcohol could be obtained. On calling there, I was, if I remember correctly, allowed one or perhaps two bottles of wine plus a half or third of a bottle of spirits. The only spirits available then just happened to be Bols Gin. Although I was not particularly keen at that time, I decided to accept what was on sale.

I wasn't sure that I still had the Gin, so I said nothing to Anita at that time. However, on returning to the ship, I found that it was still there, and intact. I returned in the evening and quietly handed it over to both Anita's great pleasure and her mother's thankful delight. They then insisted that I join her in sampling a little of the beverage.

I was ashore on Wednesday morning and afternoon, during which time I visited the souvenir shop, and said goodbye to all our new-found friends. We cast off from the wharf at 8:30 p.m. on 4th July and sailed out to the most tremendous and heart-warming send-off ever experienced. It seemed as if the entire population was on the wharf, shouting, waving and cheering, plus the occupants of cars and lorries sounding their horns.

Fig.35 Author with Canadian host 'Kay'

As we moved out to sea, the captain gave our final farewell with three loud blasts from the ship's horn. Then we had, somewhat reluctantly, to resume our duties. Half an hour later, the captain came into the radio room and handed me two letters, one he had received from the agents in Campbellton. One was a message stating that no private telegrams were yet to be transmitted from the ship. The other, however, was a personal one from my father which I was more than happy to receive.

We had a calm sea but with a cold wind on Thursday. Because of our position, it was back to taking bearings once again. At about 12:15 a.m. on Friday morning, the bridge was able to see the lights of St. Pierre and Cape Race, but in the afternoon, we were into thick fog. I was having to take bearings again, plus transmitting our position, course, and speed. In the early evening, we passed quite close to a schooner with her fishing dory boats around her. Later, at 11 p.m., we heard the sound of a ship's horn, but there was no transmission from her reporting her position, although I had sent one less than an hour earlier.

Because of the thick fog, I was called from my bunk at 4 a.m., and again at 6 a.m., to take further bearings. This continued at intervals during the day, sending out our position, course and speed (PCS). At one point, I was called by an unknown ship asking if we had received their PCS. We hadn't, so it was re-sent. They were bound for St. Johns but had stopped engines because of the fog.

In the early hours of Sunday, I was soaked once again by water coming through the deckhead. Later in the day, the wind shifted northwards and the fog slowly began to clear. From an overheard message, I learned that we should have been calling up every eight hours to a shore station, at least until we had passed forty-three degrees west. We were now nearly 46W, but I joined the queue of the many others trying to raise the station. As a result, it was nearly an hour before I was able to pass my message. Finally, on Thursday, we received a message giving our destination as Liverpool.

Next day at 9 a.m., I received a message requesting any ship which was within one hundred miles of the position, 53.50 N, 18.35 W at 7 p.m. tomorrow to report their PCS. After considerable difficulty in raising a land station, I was eventually able to comply. Strangely, nothing ever came from it, and I still wonder what it was about. On Saturday 14th July, Italy announced they were now at war with Japan.

In the evening, the bridge picked up the lights on the Irish Coast. Confirming that my last bearing was *'spot-on'*, they gave me an ETA to send to Land's End Radio. The weather deteriorated with low visibility on Sunday, and it was quite rough throughout my 8 p.m. to midnight watch. A nearby ship sent out her PCS and I followed suit. The captain then had me taking regular bearings from midnight until 3 a.m. When I eventually got to my bunk, I found the rain had been leaking through yet again. However, only an hour and a half later, I was called out again for the rest of that day.

The weather began to clear after 6 a.m., when we drifted closer to the Irish coast, albeit with no actual sight of land. After taking more bearings, our course was altered and we made for the Skerries, off the Irish coast. From there, we then made our way to the Liverpool Bar, arriving at 6 p.m. We took on the pilot at 10 p.m., finally docking at Liverpool at 6 a.m. on Monday. We were informed that discharging of our cargo would commence at 8 a.m. and, if they could get enough workers, it should be complete in five days.

I had a hectic day writing letters, which was not helped by the fact that the typewriter was not working. Eventually completing my task by evening, I managed to catch the train to Wigan at 10:45 p.m. However, on arrival, I found there were no available seats on the Perth-bound train. There was no choice but to stand all the way to Larbert, near Stirling, before eventually getting a seat. Being so tired, I fell asleep somewhere between Stirling and Perth. On arrival at 7:15 a.m., I phoned my sister, Cora, at New Fowlis, to tell her I would arrive there on the bus at about 9 a.m. After something to eat, I fell asleep until 1 p.m. I was back in Perth again in the afternoon to get some petrol coupons for the car.

I got the car on the road on Sunday, and we took a drive up to Crianlarich and back by Loch Tay and Aberfeldy. It was marvellous to be out in the Scottish countryside again. During that week, most of my evenings were spent with Betty, and then, on the following Sunday, we had a drive once again through the Sma' Glen, Aberfeldy, Logierait and Pitlochry to Kirkmichael and back via Blairgowrie. It was magic.

The next evening, Betty and I were invited for supper in Methven, to the house of Miss Craig, a close family friend who was a teacher in Methven School. My father had been Headmaster there for twenty-one years. When we were at the point of sitting down to our meal, there was a knock on the door. It turned out to be the local policeman, Constable Wilson, bringing a message for me. A telegram had arrived at home telling me to report back to the ship by '*noon tomorrow*'. As Miss Craig did not have a telephone at the time, my father had rung Constable Wilson to ask if he would kindly pass on this urgent message, such were the limited communication options back then.

The deadline, of course, was impossible. The first available train from Perth did not leave until 8:40 a.m. the next morning. I left early on Tuesday by car accompanied by my father and, by pre-arrangement, picked up Betty so that she could drive the car back home. Our speed of progress was troubling me quite a bit when the car engine began spluttering and had to be coaxed along. Thankfully, I managed to catch the train, which arrived in Liverpool at 4:50 p.m.

I was very relieved to find Thomas awaiting me at the station. However, he then told me that whilst Winsum was supposed to be sailing early the next morning, this had been changed to the following day. After waiting in a taxi queue for half an hour, we realised that we would not reach the ship in time for dinner. I put my case in left luggage, and we proceeded to Reace's for a meal. Then, making the most of the opportunity, it was on to the Empire to see a show, before returning on board at 10:30 p.m. It was midnight before I eventually, and very thankfully, got into my bunk after what seemed to have been a very long day.

On Wednesday 1st August, I met the new second R/O, by the name of Cotton, who had been appointed to replace Jones. We left the dock at 4:30 a.m. on Thursday, and after initial adjustment of the compasses, we finally dropped the pilot at 8:30 a.m. and sailed out into the fog. I was back taking regular bearings until 5:30 p.m. when it suddenly cleared. The coastlines of both Ireland and Scotland were now visible. In the early hours of Friday, we encountered more fog and I was taking bearings every half hour between 7:30 a.m. and 3:30 p.m. Eventually, the bridge could see a point on the Isle of Skye. Going on late watch at eight o'clock, we remained close to the Scottish coast. It was a lovely clear evening and the mountains behind were a grand sight.

We had a calm passage through the Pentland Firth on Saturday. In the afternoon, we received our first chargeable message from our agents in South Shields, requesting our ETA. Coming on watch at 8 p.m. to relieve Cotton, he was unaware whether he had received a reply or acknowledgement of his answers to the messages. It took me some time before I was able to raise a Shore Station to inform our ETA and receive an acknowledgement. We arrived at South Shields at 10 a.m. on Sunday. On asking the old man if there was any chance of my getting home, he said to 'wait until tomorrow.' Next day we learned that work on the ship would not start until Wednesday. 'Because of Bank Holidays', was the reason I was given. I was able to get away at 2:30 p.m., but the second and third R/Os were told to split their leave as there had to be one R/O on board. I reached Perth in time to catch the last bus, but unfortunately, had to wake up the family at Fowlis on my arrival.

While still at home on Wednesday 15th August, I was wakened at 8:15 a.m. by my mother with great news.

'*The war is over!*', she declared, referring to the Japanese surrender.

Later, I travelled to Perth to get a new licence and insurance for the car. Unfortunately, the office was closed, requiring a return journey on Friday. Betty and I were able to attend a fete in Methven on Saturday. What a contrast to again experience normal, everyday life.

On Wednesday 22nd August, I received a recall to South Shields. Later in the day, however, Betty and I went over to Jackstone Farm, Bankfoot, to spend the evening with the Ewan family, friends of Betty. Next day, I left home at 2:15 p.m. and it was 9:15 p.m. when I arrived back on board Winsum.

We sailed from the Tyne at 12:15 a.m. on Saturday 25th August. At the Bar, we passed the Dutch liner Oranje Fontein and greeted each other by dipping flags. We passed the entrance to the Tay estuary around 1 a.m. the next morning and, shortly afterwards, our course was changed to an easterly direction. It turned out to be a beautiful day and we passed many ships as we sailed in a swept channel through the still-present minefields. Although buoys marked the sides of the safe channel, we heard of a Dutch liner named Chris Huygens, reporting an *'explosion'* and, *'sinking slowly!'*

At 8 a.m. on Monday, we sighted the Norwegian coast. When nearing the shore at about 2 p.m., we turned off at a lighthouse to follow another buoyed passage. On Tuesday, we had a pilot on board from early morning until mid-forenoon. Later that evening, another pilot took us through the channel past Copenhagen. On Thursday (30th), the weather deteriorated, resulting in my having to take bearings once more.

Friday was the Dutch Queen Wilhelmina's birthday. We were now in the Gulf of Bothnia, between Sweden and Finland, and it was turning colder. At 10 a.m. I contacted the Swedish Shore Station Härnösand, and in return, received a message giving our destination as Mo, near to the top of the Gulf.

Going on deck at 7:30 a.m. on Saturday, I was surprised to find that we were only just approaching our destination. It had been estimated previously that we would arrive by 1 a.m. All was explained when the pilot came aboard after midnight. He disclosed that there were two places named 'Mo', and ours was some thirty to forty miles further on than originally believed. When the mate recounted this, he said it was, *'thirty or forty odd miles ...'*. This reminded me with a smile, of the previous whaling story involving the word 'odd' and its identical pronunciation of a Norwegian surname 'Aad'.

We finally got tied up at 8:30 a.m., on a beautiful day, but with a nip in the air. There was very little to be seen ashore in the way of habitation. On coming aboard, the ship's agent said there was little more than a sawmill and a small second-hand shop. Unfortunately, this proved accurate. The countryside was very flat and covered with pine forests. Off-shore, there was a scattering of small islands, which helped somewhat to relieve the otherwise bleak outlook.

The nearest town was called Umea and could be reached by an irregular bus service in about three hours or so. However, we learned that whilst in Sweden, we were only allowed to draw twenty kronor per man per week. I was told the unfortunate story today about Cotton asking Thomas where he could get a bucket of hot water. He was told to go down to the engine room, where he would see *'a bucket and a tap'*. All he had to do was *'turn on the tap.'* Unfortunately, the poor lad turned on the fuel tap, resulting in him being sprayed all over with the foul-smelling liquid.

Sunday 2nd September 1945 started off dull and cold with a strong wind, but it became another momentous day. I was able to report from the radio that stated, *'the 'Japs' had signed the agreement of surrender on-board the US battleship Missouri in Tokyo harbour'*.

The following morning, Thomas was going to visit Umea, so I drew my first kronor allowance so he could buy things for me. Cotton was also proposing to catch the same bus but missed it. However, he later hitched a ride on the van which collected the ship's laundry. Next afternoon, Thomas and I went ashore to see if we could purchase anything at the second-hand shop. It proved very difficult, partly because we couldn't speak Swedish, and the shop lady couldn't speak English. In fact, there was very little to buy anyway. We were not able to buy cakes because we did not have the necessary food coupons. All we could get were four small homemade pastries and five small pears, all of which did not require coupons.

The bad weather returned on Wednesday with a very strong wind. During the forenoon, our anchors dragged, causing us to drift down on another ship close by, and crushing our dinghy. A larger tug arrived later and we were moved in the evening so that we lay head-on to the wind, and had fresh hawsers connected to shore.

I learned on Thursday morning that Cotton had arrived back on board late the previous evening. He had been missing since Monday. According to the stories of his exploits, as told down in the mess room, it was reckoned that he must have had a high old time. His solitary purchase was a small radio. The captain and chief engineer travelled to Umea today. They were accompanied by the local stevedore, whose purpose was to act as interpreter and guide. Their aim was to replenish their wardrobes, prior to their imminent return to wives and families, after a considerable six-year absence.

Letters arrived on Friday, but none for me. Cotton left for town once again, notably fully dressed in uniform. Apparently, his new radio was not working. On Saturday, our laundry was returned, but was all mixed up, and some items were missing, including my good sweater. The old man held another one of his famous parties this evening, after receiving six ladies and three men aboard. Thomas told me on Sunday (9th) that he had eaten ashore the previous day, and the main course consisted of horse flesh. He seemed to think it tasted alright, but I didn't think that I could have faced it.

On Monday, to keep ourselves busy, the third mate, Thomas and I rowed out to one of the small islands off-shore. Next evening, we were witness to a lovely display of the Aurora Borealis, or Northern Lights. The Swedish ship Kulmarsund sailed out during Wednesday morning and another Swedish ship arrived the following morning to occupy their vacant berth.

We finished loading part of our cargo here at 4:30 p.m. We eventually left Mo at 1 a.m. on Friday morning, 14th September, and arrived at Domsjo further down the Gulf at 6:30 a.m. Loading of additional cargo of wood began at 10 a.m. We were told that we could now draw up to one-third of two weeks' wages.

Come Sunday, with eighty kronor in my pocket, I accompanied Veldhuis on a walk into the town. Our sight-seeing was swiftly curtailed at 4 p.m. when the heavens opened up with torrential rain, thunder and lightning.

We hurriedly got a taxi back to Winsum. In any case, the captain had another party in the evening, but unusually, it broke up before 9 p.m. With everything still in short supply, bartering remained vigorous on-board. Buyl, who was desperate for a smoke, offered me two bars of chocolate in return for one cigar, which I was glad to accept.

Some food coupons were then made available. So, on Wednesday, in the company of the third mate and engineer, I was again ashore for another walk-around. However, the only money spent was for having tea and cakes, using some of the food coupons that we had received.

Arriving back on board at 6 p.m., I lay down for a couple of hours before going across to an adjoining Danish ship. Thomas had told me they were eager to exchange kronor for English notes. One of the crew readily gave me eighty-five kronor for my £5 note.

Fig.36 Swedish Food Ration Coupons

I heard on the radio later that the infamous Lord Haw-Haw (aka William Joyce), who broadcast Nazi propaganda from Germany, had been sentenced to death.

After breakfast on Thursday, I visited a nearby Swedish ship, the SS Gallio, and exchanged another three pounds sterling for fifty kronor. I then set off to do some shopping in the company of Veldhuis and Cotton. After reaching the town, we decided to go our separate ways. I was very keen to purchase a double-barrelled shotgun and visited the first gun shop I found. There, I learned that a licence was required before a purchase could be made. I then decided to try the Police Headquarters. On arrival, I explained my mission and got a very courteous reception, before being taken to the office of the Inspector in charge.

Once again, the language barrier was a bit of a problem, but the atmosphere lightened considerably when he requested my name. I then thought to myself, '*I am going to be alright here*'. On giving the reply, 'Anderson', the Inspector threw himself back in his chair and roared with laughter at the thought of a Scotsman having what he considered to be a Swedish surname.

When he had recovered, the Inspector then had some difficulty in determining exactly what type of weapon I was wanting to acquire until, at one point, he suddenly pulled open the top drawer of his desk. He then placed his right hand into the drawer before smartly withdrawing a pistol which he then proceeded to point straight at me.

After my initial shock, I got to my feet and, like a game of charades, held out both arms as if holding a normal, full-sized shotgun. Then, with the use of two fingers, and in continued silence, attempted to indicate side-by-side twin barrels. The message finally got through to the relief of all concerned. Alas, despite all this, and even with a letter (of reference) from the ship's captain, the answer to my request was,

"I am sorry, but no."

We shook hands and he wished me *'good luck'*. Whether for my continued search, or in general, I knew not. However, leaving the Police Station, I decided that I would purchase something else with the money. I duly ended up with some less lethal items, namely, two alarm clocks, a pair of pliers and a few small souvenirs. On my return to the ship, I learned that the third mate and Cotton had bartered at a shop, getting radios in exchange for cigarettes.

I was going to exchange fifty of my remaining sixty kronor, but decided to return to town on Friday to purchase a radio, after seeing Cotton returning with one for the third mate as they had arranged the day before. He informed me that the shop had only one left, so I wasted no time and purchased it for forty kronor plus one hundred cigarettes. Next day, I returned ashore with Thomas in the forenoon to purchase a valve for the chief engineer's radio and an alarm clock for the second mate. My only purchase was the price of a haircut. On my return, I was happy to receive letters from my mother and Betty. The chief engineer had received another letter from Holland which bore the news that his eldest son had pleurisy and had to stay in bed for nine months.

Before we sailed out at 3:30 p.m., Customs officers came on-board again, just as they had done before we left Mo. It turned very cold at night, and I was called to take bearings at midnight and at 6 a.m. This was later followed at 8 a.m. when I had to continue at half-hourly intervals until, eventually, the bridge sighted a marker buoy.

We were now sailing between Gotland and the Swedish mainland on a beautiful clear Monday morning. I contacted the pilot station at Trelleborg, giving them our position and ETA. When off-watch, I spent some time cleaning and adjusting the car radio which I had purchased in Quebec. I was more than delighted with its performance. We picked up the pilot at 10 a.m. on Tuesday and the old man was very pleased that he had details of our route as requested in the message I sent earlier. Later, the old man decided that he wanted another message sent to Copenhagen, requesting further information.

It then transpired that Cotton heard a Station 'OXC' transmitting a list of ships for which they had messages. Unfortunately, he failed to contact OXC to receive the message. I was then immediately summoned by the old man to find that Cotton was on the wrong waveband. After correcting this, I called up OXC and received our message. Then, at 7 p.m., within sight of the German coast, we dropped anchor in lovely weather.

The German pilot came on board at 11 a.m. on Wednesday, 26th September and took us into Kiel, where we anchored until 3:30 p.m. There was a pathway running along the side of the Kiel Canal and in clear view of the ship. The chief engineer was on deck and when he saw a male cyclist passing by, he shouted out,

"Look at that 'B......' German, - he's riding my bicycle!"

We then proceeded through the Canal, and into the North Sea later in the evening. We learned today that all British members of the crew are to be discharged and returned to England after our arrival in Amsterdam.

On Thursday forenoon, we passed the SS Hilversum and exchanged greetings by blowing ships' horns. The captain then gave me a long message to send to his opposite number. This was replied to and received by Colin Thomas when he took over from me at midday. The gist of the reply was that the Hilversum had bunkered and taken on stores at Hull before returning home. It was now bound for the Umea area of Sweden which we had recently left.

After coming off watch at midnight, and trying to get some sleep, I was eventually forced to get up and terminate a long *tête-à-tête* being conducted between Thomas and his opposite number on the Hilversum. The Dutch pilot came on board at 11 a.m. on Friday and we tied up in drizzling rain at about 2:30 p.m. beside the SS H. Tegner and SS Trompenberg. Coming through the last lock, a man standing there had spoken to the chief mate who was astonished to find that they had been schoolmates twenty-one years before.

As soon as we had tied up, a party of men and one lady from the owners and agents came aboard and sat down to dinner with us. They spoke very excitedly about their wartime experiences, and although I could speak little more than a word or two of the language, I was able to understand a fair amount of what they were saying.

I remember the lady saying their greatest joy was when RAF Bombers flew over after their liberation and dropped food parcels which included chocolate. This comment was heartily supported by the menfolk. They obviously enjoyed their meal, eating almost ravenously and clearing their plates of every scrap of food. At the end, as the plates were being taken away by the steward, I then felt quite embarrassed seeing the cut-off fat still lying on mine.

A representative from Radio Holland came on board to receive my report and said that the ship would be reverting to Single Operator status. I signified that this was no problem as myself and my two R/Os all wished to leave in any case. The first of the Dutch crew to get leave set off complete with baggage at 4:30 p.m. I wondered what awaited them on reaching their homes. Great joy for some no doubt, but possibly tears for others.

On Saturday 29th September, the first and second mates and the third and fourth engineers left the ship at

9:30 a.m. to return home. The captain returned from his home at midday accompanied by his wife and daughter. A sailor, who had returned from the company's office, told Thomas that he had overheard a conversation there. It was mentioned that the British crew members would be leaving for home on Wednesday. Later, when the captain came to show a party of visitors to the radio room, I told him what I had heard. He was very surprised and replied,

"I will see about that".

He then added that if I personally wanted to stay, he would do his utmost to keep me on. However, on being told that I wished to return home, he said that he quite understood, but was very sorry that was the case.

The captain returned on board on Monday 1st October from the weekend at home, but still had not received any news about our departure. The second mate also returned for the day and accompanied Thomas and me to the Radio Holland office. On our return to the ship, we had Cotton quite worried when we said that he had to stay with the ship on his own. On Wednesday, I learned that one of the crew had sold a second pair of shoes for money, to someone on the quay. When I thought of what those poor people had come through during their years of occupation, it was somewhat sickening to me to hear of this.

I received a letter from my father on Thursday, with an enclosed telegram which he had originally sent to me via the Central Telegraph Office in London. However, it had been subsequently returned to him. The telegram bore the Central Office date stamp of September 18th and contained the message, '*Salvesen offers you post as chief on Sevilla Whaling. Sails 28 September*'. I was quite taken aback by this unexpected opportunity from my former employers. However, as the Expedition had now already sailed on its way to the Antarctic, my chance of a return voyage had literally sailed.

However, I was soon brought back to my senses when the agent came on-board at 5:30 p.m. with a note saying that we were to be ready with baggage to leave on Monday morning, 8th October, first thing!

Going ashore on Friday to post some letters, I also booked seats at a cinema for the evening show. Next day, whilst on deck, I saw a thin, poor-looking young lad standing on a barge in his clogs. I thought he was so sad-looking that I decided to search my cabin in search of something I could give him. I duly returned with a shirt and a jacket which I offered to him. He seemed reluctant at first, possibly thinking I was expecting payment, but his face lit up when he realised they were a gift, and he gratefully accepted them. It made my day.

As Sunday was to be my last day on-board, I cleaned up generally, both in my cabin and the radio room, for what would be the last time, and then packaged what belongings I still possessed.

Next morning, we were picked up by a decrepit-looking small bus, which very noisily chugged along en route to Rotterdam at a speed which could not have, at any point, exceeded ten miles an hour. This despite the fact, of course, that there are no hills to climb in that part of the country. As my diary notes stopped from that day, I cannot say how long the short journey took, but it certainly seemed to last a long two or three hours. Suffice it to say that when I descended from that vehicle, I felt as if I had come out of a threshing machine, and I had the most terrible headache.

For the remainder of my story, I have to rely on memory. Unfortunately, in respect of my journey home, the worst was not over. We were led to a ferry boat of some description, and then down below to a large open deck. This was where we had to sleep, lying cheek to jowl. The boat was over-crowded with servicemen and women from all services.

I do not remember where or when we arrived in England, but I do remember that I did arrive home on Tuesday 9th October, very, very tired, but to a great 'welcome home'.

I later received my 'Record of Service' with Salvesen's and a 'Merchant Navy Service Discharge Certificate', and so ended my six years at sea, from October 1939 to October 1945.

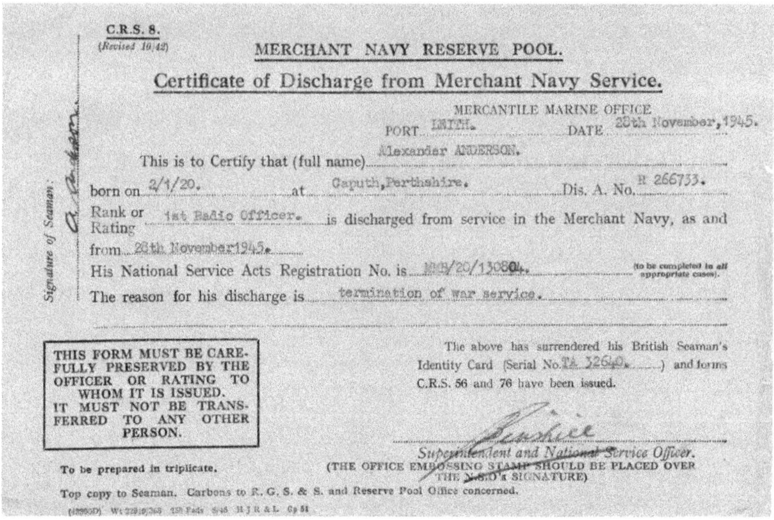

C.R.S. 8.
(Revised 10/42)

MERCHANT NAVY RESERVE POOL.

Certificate of Discharge from Merchant Navy Service.

MERCANTILE MARINE OFFICE
PORT LEITH. DATE 28th November, 1945.

This is to Certify that (full name) Alexander ANDERSON.
born on 2/1/20. at Caputh, Perthshire. Dis. A. No. R 266733.
Rank or Rating 1st Radio Officer. is discharged from service in the Merchant Navy, as and from 28th November 1945.
His National Service Acts Registration No. is [illegible]/20/130804. (to be completed in all appropriate cases).
The reason for his discharge is termination of war service.

Signature of Seaman:

THIS FORM MUST BE CAREFULLY PRESERVED BY THE OFFICER OR RATING TO WHOM IT IS ISSUED.
IT MUST NOT BE TRANSFERRED TO ANY OTHER PERSON.

The above has surrendered his British Seaman's Identity Card (Serial No. TA 32640.) and forms C.R.S. 56 and 76 have been issued.

Superintendent and ~~National Service~~ Officer.

To be prepared in triplicate.

(THE OFFICE EMBOSSING ~~STAMP~~ SHOULD BE PLACED OVER THE ~~N.S.O~~'s SIGNATURE)

Top copy to Seaman. Carbons to R. G. S. & S. and Reserve Pool Office concerned.

Fig.37 MN Termination of War Service Discharge Certificate

Now, as my story ends, and I conclude some fifty-two years on, I still remember the happy memories as well as the sad, and give thanks for being spared to come through it all, from *'Hunter to Hunted'*!

~ END ~